Tipping recommendations

It's not very customary to give tips in Denmark. Hotel and restaurant bills always include service; tip only if special services have been rendered. It is also included in restaurant bills, though a little extra is frequently added if you are satisfied with the meal and the service.

HOTEL	
Service charge, bill	15% included
Porter, per bag	2–3 crowns
Bellboy, errand	4–5 crowns
Maid	optional
Doorman, hails cab	5 crowns
RESTAURANT	
Service charge, bill	15% included
Waiter	optional
Cloakroom attendant	charges posted
Lavatory attendant	2 crowns
Taxi driver	included
Barber/Women's hairdresser	none
Tour guide	optional
Theatre usher	none

BERLITZ PHRASE BOOKS

World's bestselling phrase books feature not only expressions and vocabulary you'll need, but also travel tips, useful facts and pronunciation throughout. The handiest and most readable conversation aid available.

Arabic	French	Polish
Chinese	German	Portuguese
Danish	Greek	Russian
Dutch	Hebrew	Serbo-Croatian
European (14 languages)	Hungarian	Spanish
	Italian	Lat.-Am. Spanish
European Menu Reader	Japanese	Swahili
	Korean	Swedish
Finnish	Norwegian	Turkish

BERLITZ CASSETTEPAKS

The above-mentioned titles are also available combined with a cassette to help you improve your accent. A helpful miniscript is included containing the complete text of the dual language hi-fi recording.

BERLITZ®

DANISH
FOR TRAVELLERS

By the staff of Berlitz Guides

Library of Congress Catalog Card Number: 75-11282

Revised edition
11th printing 1989

Printed in Switzerland

Berlitz Guides
Avenue d'Ouchy 61
1000 Lausanne 6, Switzerland

Preface

You are about to visit Denmark. Our aim has been to produce a practical phrase book to help you on your trip.

In preparing this book we took into account a wealth of suggestions from phrase book users around the world. The accent is on helping the traveller in practical, every-day situations.

The contents are logically arranged so you can find the right phrase at the moment you need it.

Danish for Travellers features:

● all the phrases and supplementary vocabulary you'll need on your trip

● complete phonetic transcription throughout, enabling you to pronounce every word correctly

● special panels showing replies your listener might like to give you: just hand him the book and let him point to the appropriate phrase. This is particularly useful in certain difficult situations (trouble with the car, at the doctors's, etc.)

● a wide range of travel facts, hints and useful practical information, providing valuable insight into life in Denmark

● a tipping chart (see inside back-cover) and a reference section in the back of the book

● an introduction to some basics of Danish grammar

Certain sections will be particularly appreciated by travellers: the extensive "Eating Out" chapter which explains what's on the menu, in the soup and under the sauce, with translations, and the complete "Shopping Guide" which enables you to be almost as specific and selective as you would be at home. Trouble with the car? Turn to the mechanic's manual with its dual-language terms. Feeling ill? Our medical section provides the most rapid communication possible between you and the doctor.

To make the most of *Danish for Travellers*, we suggest that you start with the "Guide to Pronunciation". Then go on to "Some Basic Expressions". This not only gives you a basic vocabulary, it also helps you get used to pronouncing the language.

We're particularly grateful to Mrs. R. Caspar, Mrs. M. Cursoli and Mr. D. Pulman for their help in the preparation of this book and to Dr. T.J.A. Bennett and Miss L. Kristensen who devised the phonetic transcription. We also wish to thank the Danish National Travel Office for its assistance.

We shall be very pleased to receive any comments, criticisms and suggestions that you think may help us in preparing future editions.

Thank you. Have a good trip.

Throughout this book, the symbols illustrated here indicate small sections where phrases have been compiled that your foreign listener might like to say to *you*. If you don't understand him, give him the book and let him point to the phrase in his language. The English translation is just beside it.

Basic grammar

The Danish and English languages are historically closely related. This can be seen most clearly in the vocabulary, e.g. *arm,* arm, *under,* under, *land,* country, *frost,* frost, etc. Danish is comfortingly like English in having few word endings. If the existence of two genders seems to complicate matters, remember that most nouns are of common gender, and a mistake here will rarely lead to misunderstanding.

A relatively simple grammatical structure, combined with a somewhat familiar vocabulary, makes it possible for an English-speaker to acquire a working knowledge of Danish without too much difficulty.

Here is the briefest possible outline of the essential features of Danish grammar.

Nouns and articles

All nouns in Danish are either common or neuter in gender. (Although most nouns are of common gender, it's best to learn each together with its article.)

1. Indefinite article (a/an)

A/an is expressed by **en** with common nouns and by **et** with neuter nouns.

Indefinite plurals are formed by adding **-e** or **-er** to the singular.

	singular		plural	
common gender	*en* **bil**	a car	**bil**er	cars
neuter gender	*et* **hus**	a house	**hus**e	houses

Some nouns remain unchanged in the plural.

singular: *et* **rum**   a room   plural: **rum**   rooms

2. Definite article (the)

Where we in English say "the car", the Danes say the equivalent of "car-the", i.e. they tag the definite article onto the end of the noun.

In the singular, common nouns take an **-en** ending, neuter nouns an **-et** ending. In the plural, both take an **-(e)ne** or **-(er)ne** ending.

	singular		plural	
common gender	**bil**en	the car	**bil**(er)ne	the cars
neuter gender	**tog**et	the train	**tog**(e)ne	the trains

3. Possessives

The possessive form is shown by adding **-s**.

ugens **slutning**	the end of the week
Jørgens **broder**	George's brother

Adjectives

1. They usually precede the noun.

2. In certain circumstances, the adjective takes an ending.

Indefinite form:

singular { common nouns: adjective remains unchanged;
neuter nouns: adjective takes a **-t** ending.

plural { with both common and neuter nouns, the adjective takes an **-e** ending

	singular		plural	
common	**en dansk bil**	a Danish car	**danske bil**er	Danish cars
neuter	**et stort hus**	a big house	**store hus**e	big houses

Definite form:

The adjective takes an **-e** ending everywhere, with both common and neuter nouns, in both singular and plural. However, in this definite usage, **den** must be placed in front of the adjective in the case of common nouns in the singular, **det** in the case of singular neuter nouns and **de** with any plural.

	singular		plural	
common	*den* **danske bil**	the Danish car	*de* **danske biler**	the Danish cars
neuter	*det* **store hus**	the big house	*de* **store huse**	the big houses

Demonstrative adjectives

	common	neuter	plural
this/these	**denne**	**dette**	**disse**
that/those	**den**	**det**	**de**

denne **bil**   this car   *dette* **hus**   this house

Possessive adjectives

	common	neuter	plural
my	**min**	**mit**	**mine**
your (familiar; see note on next page)	**din**	**dit**	**dine**
our	**vor**	**vort**	**vore**
his		**hans**	
her		**hendes**	
its		**dens/dets***	
their		**deres**	
your (familiar; see note on next page)		**jeres**	
your (formal; see note on next page)		**Deres**	

* Use **dens** if "it" is of common gender, and **dets** if "it" is neuter.

Personal pronouns

	subject	object
I	jeg	mig
you (familiar; see note below)	du	dig
he	han	ham
she	hun	hende
it	den/det*	den/det*
we	vi	os
you (familiar; see note below)	I	jer
you (formal; see note below)	De	Dem
they	de	dem

Note: Like many other languages, Danish has two forms for "you" and "your". The personal pronoun **du** (plural **I**) and its corresponding possessive adjectives **din**, **dit**, **dine** (plural **jeres)** are used when talking to relatives, close friends and children and between young people. The personal pronoun **Des** (plural **Dem**) and its corresponding possessive adjective **Deres** is used in all other cases.

Verbs

Here we are concerned only with the infinitive, present tense and imperative.

The infinitive of Danish verbs generally ends in **-er, -o, -ø** or **-å,** and is preceded by **at** (corresponding to English "to").

at rejse	to travel	at gå	to walk
at tro	to believe	at spise	to eat

The present tense drops the **at** and adds **-r** to the infinitive. This form remains unchanged for all persons.

jeg rejser	I travel	jeg går	I walk
jeg tror	I believe	jeg spiser	I eat

The imperative is exactly the same form as the stem of the verb.

rejs!	travel!	gå!	walk!
tro!	believe!	spis!	eat!

* Use **den** if "it" is of common gender, and **det** if "it" is neuter.

GRAMMAR

Here are three useful auxiliary verbs:

	to be	to have	to be able to, can
infinitive	**at være**	**at have**	**at kunne**
present tense (same form for all persons)	**jeg er**, etc.	**jeg har**, etc.	**jeg kan**, etc.
imperative	**vær!**	**hav!**	—

Adverbs

Adverbs are generally formed by adding **-t** to the corresponding adjective.

> **Hun går hurtigt.**　　　　　She walks quickly.

Negatives

Negatives are formed by inserting the word **ikke** after the verb:

> **Jeg taler dansk.**　　　　　I speak Danish.
> **Jeg taler** *ikke* **dansk.**　　I do not speak Danish.

Questions

Questions are formed by reversing the order of the subject and verb:

> **Du ser bilen.**　　　　　You see the car.
> **Ser du bilen?**　　　　　Do you see the car?

There is/there are

Der er is employed for both "there is" and "there are".

> *Der er* **mange turister.**　　There are many tourists.

It is

> *Det er* **varmt i dag.**　　　It is warm today.

GRAMMAR

Guide to pronunciation

This and the following chapter are intended to make you familiar with the phonetic transcription we have devised and to help you get used to the sounds of Danish.

As a minimum vocabulary for your trip, we've selected a number of basic words and phrases under the title "Some basic expressions" (pages 16–21).

An outline of the spelling and sounds of Danish

You'll find the pronunciation of the Danish letters and sounds explained below, as well as the symbols we're using for them in the transcriptions.

The imitated pronunciation should be read as if it were English except for any special rules set out below. Of course, the sounds of any two languages are never exactly the same; but if you follow carefully the indications supplied here, you'll have no difficulty in reading our transcriptions in such a way as to make yourself understood.

Letters written in bold type should be stressed.

Consonants

Letter	Approximate pronunciation	Symbol	Example	
b, c, f, g, l, m, n, v	as in English			
d	1) when at the end of the word after a vowel, or between a vowel and unstressed **e** or **i**, like **th** in **this**. (It's sometimes silent at the end of a word.)	dh	**med**	maydh
	2) otherwise, as in English	d	**dale**	**daa**ler

PRONUNCIATION

g	1) at the beginning of a word or syllable, as in **go**	g	**glas**	glahss
	2) when at the end of a word after a long vowel or before unstressed **e**, usually like **y** in **yet** (though occasionally rather like **ch** in Scottish **loch**); sometimes mute after **a**, **e**, **o**	y	**sige**	sēēyer
hv	like **v** in **view**	v	**hvor**	vōār
j, hj	like **y** in **yet**	y	**ja**	yǣ
k	1) between vowels, generally like **g** in **go** (unvoiced)	g	**ikke**	igger
	2) otherwise like **k** in **kite**	k	**kaffe**	kahfer
l	always as in **leaf**, never as in **bell**	l	**vel**	vehl
ng	as in **sing**, never as in **finger**, unless **n** and **g** are in separate syllables	ng	**ingen**	ingern
		ngg	**ingrediens**	inggraydeeehnss
p	1) between vowels, generally like **b** in **bit** (unvoiced)	b	**stoppe**	stobber
	2) otherwise like **p** in **pill**	p	**pude**	poodher
r	pronounced in the back of the throat, as in French, at the beginnings of words, but otherwise often omitted	r	**rose**	rōāsser
s	always as in **see** (*never* as in **rise**)	s/ss	**skål**	skawl
			ventesal	vehnderssaal
sj	usually like **sh** in **sheet** (but may also be pronounced like the **ss y** in **pass you**)	sh	**sjælden**	shehlern
t	1) between vowels, generally like **d** in **do** (unvoiced)	d	**lytte**	lewder
	2) otherwise like **t** in **to** (at the end of a word often mute)	t	**torsk**	toarsk

Note: The letter **d** is not pronounced in **nd** and **ld** at the end of a word or syllable (*guld* = **gool**), or before unstressed **e** or before **t** or **s** in the same syllable (*plads* = **plahss**).

PRONUNCIATION

Vowels

A vowel is generally long in stressed syllables when it's the final letter or followed by only one consonant. If followed by two or more consonants, or in unstressed syllables, the vowel is generally short.

a	1) when long, like **a** in car	aa	**klare**	**klaar**er
	2) when short, more like **a** in cart	ah	**hat**	haht
	3) you will also hear, as alternatives to the above, a more or less "flat" pronunciation of **a**, which can be like a in hat, or tend towards e in let; it can be long or short	ǣ æ ai eh	**ja** **tak** **tale** **kan**	y**ǣ** t**æk** **tai**ler k**eh**n
e	1) when long, the same quality as **a** in plate, but longer, and a pure vowel, *not* a diphthong	āȳ	**flere**	fl**āȳ**rer
	2) when short, somewhere between the **a** in plate and the **i** in hit	ay	**fedt**	f**ay**d
	3) when short, also like **e** in met	eh	**let**	l**eh**d
	4) when unstressed, like **a** in above	er*	**hjælpe**	**yeh**lper
i	1) when long, like **ee** in bee	ēē	**ile**	**ēē**ler
	2) when short, like **ee** in meet or more between **a** in plate and **i** in pin	ee i	**liter** **drikke**	**lee**derr **dri**gger
o	1) when long, like **oa** in boat, but a pure vowel, *not* a diphthong	ōa	**pol**	p**ōa**l
	2) when short, more or less the same quality of sound	oa	**bonde**	**boa**ner

PRONUNCIATION

---

* The r should not be pronounced when reading this transcription.

	3) when short, also like **o** in l**o**t	o	**godt**	god
u	1) when long, like **oo** in p**oo**l	o͞o	**frue**	fr**o͞o**er
	2) when short, like **oo** in l**oo**t	oo	**nu**	noo
y	put your tongue in the position for the **ee** of b**ee**, but round your lips as for the **oo** of p**oo**l	ew	**nyde** **lytte**	n**e͞w**dher **lew**der
æ	1) when long, vowel quality fluctuates between that of **ai** in **ai**r and **ai** in t**ai**lor	ai	**sæbe**	**sai**ber
	2) when short, like **e** in g**e**t	eh	**ægte**	**ehg**ter
	3) next to **r** it sounds more like the **a** of h**a**t; can be long or short	ǣ æ	**ære** **ært**	**ǣ**rer **æ**rt
å	1) when long, like **aw** in s**aw**	aw	**åben**	**aw**bern
	2) when short, like **o** in **o**n	o	**ånd**	on
ø	like **ur** in f**ur**, but with the lips rounded; can be long or short	ūr* ur*	**frøken** **øl**	fr**ūr**gern **ur**l

Note: In or after long vowels, many Danish speakers use a glottal stop (like the Cockney pronunciation of water as wa'er). You will be understood perfectly well without it, so we have not shown this distinctive sound in our transcriptions.

Diphthongs

av, af	like **ow** in n**ow**	ow	**hav**	how
ej, ij, eg	like **igh** in s**igh**	igh	**nej**	nigh
ev	like **e** in g**e**t followed by a short **oo** sound	eh°°	**levned**	**leh°°**nerdh
ou, ov	like **o** in g**o**t followed by a short **oo** sound	o°°	**sjov**	sho°°
øi, øj	like **oi** in **oi**l	oi	**øje**	**oi**er
øv	like **ur** in h**ur**t followed by a short **oo** sound	ur°°*	**søvnig**	**sur°°**nee

---
* The **r** should not be pronounced when reading this transcription.

PRONUNCIATION

Some basic expressions

Yes.	Ja.	yæ
No.	Nej.	nigh
Please.	Vær så venlig.	vær saw **vehn**lee
Thank you.	Tak.	tæk
Thank you very much.	Mange tak.	**mahng**er tæk
That's all right.	Det er i orden.	day ayr ee **oar**dern
You're welcome.	Åh, jeg be'r.	aw yigh bāȳr

Greetings

Good morning.	Godmorgen.	goadh**mōā**ern
Good afternoon.	Goddag.	goadh**dai**
Good evening.	Godaften.	goadh**ahf**tern
Good night.	Godnat.	goadh**naht**
Good-bye.	Farvel.	fahr**vehl**
See you later.	På gensyn.	paw **gehn**sewn*
This is Mr...	Det er herr...	day ayr hehr
This is Mrs...	Det er fru...	day ayr frōō
This is Miss...	Det er frøken...	day ayr frǖrgern
I'm very pleased to meet you.	Det glæder mig at træffe Dem.	day **glaid**herr migh aht **treh**fer dehm
How are you?	Hvordan har De det?	vor**dahn** haar dee day
Very well thank's, and you?	Godt, og De?	god oa dee
How's it going?	Hvordan går det?	vor**dahn** gawr day
Excuse me.	Undskyld.	**oon**skewl
I beg your pardon.	Undskyld.	**oon**skewl
That's all right.	Det er i orden.	day ayr ee **oar**dern

* Remember, when reading our transcriptions, always to pronounce g as in "go" except in igh and ng.

Questions

Where?	Hvor?	vōar
Where's...?	Hvor er...?	vōar ayr
Where are...?	Hvor er...?	vōar ayr
How?	Hvordan?	vordahn
How much?	Hvor meget?	vōar mighert
How many?	Hvor mange?	vōar mahnger
When?	Hvornår?	vornawr
What?	Hvad?	vahdh
Why?	Hvorfor?	vorfor
Who?	Hvem?	vehm
Which?	Hvilken?	vilkern
What do you call this/that in Danish?	Hvad hedder dette på dansk?	vahdh hehdherr dehder paw dahnsk
What do you call these/those in Danish?	Hvad hedder disse på dansk?	vahdh hehdherr deesser paw dahnsk
What does this/that mean?	Hvad betyder dette?	vahdh bertēwdherr dehder dette?

Do you speak...?

Do you speak English?	Taler De engelsk?	tailerr dee ehngerlsk
Is there anyone here who speaks...?	Er der nogen her, der taler...?	ayr dayr nōāern hayr dayr tailerr
I don't speak Danish.	Jeg taler ikke dansk.	yigh tailerr igger dahnsk
Could you speak more slowly?	Tal langsommere.	tail lahngsomerrer
Could you repeat that?	Gentag det.	gehntai day
Please write it down.	Vær så venlig at skrive det ned.	vær saw vehnlee aht skrēēver day naydh
Can you translate (this) for me?	Vil De oversætte (dette) for mig?	veel dee oºᵒerrssehder (dehder) foar migh
Can you translate (this) for us?	Vil De oversætte (dette) for os?	veel dee oºᵒerrssehder (dehder) foar oss

Please point to the phrase in the book.	**Vær så venlig at udpege sætningen i bogen.**	vær saw **vehn**lee aht **oodh**pigher **seht**ningern ee b**ōā**ern
Just a minute. I'll see if I can find it in the book.	**Lige et øjeblik. Jeg skal se, om jeg kan finde den i bogen.**	**lēē**yer eht oierblik. yigh skahl s**āy** oam yigh kehn **fin**ner dehn ee b**ōā**ern
I understand.	**Jeg forstår.**	yigh for**stawr**
I don't understand.	**Jeg forstår ikke.**	yigh for**stawr igg**er
Do you understand?	**Forstår De?**	for**stawr** dee

Can...?

Can I have...?	**Kan jeg få...?**	kehn yigh faw
Can we have...	**Kan vi få...?**	kehn vee faw
Can you show me...?	**Vil De vise mig...?**	veel dee **vēē**sser migh
I can't.	**Jeg kan ikke.**	yigh kehn **igg**er
Can you tell me?	**Kan De sige mig?**	kehn dee **sēē**er migh
Can you help me?	**Kan De hjælpe mig?**	kehn dee **yehl**per migh
Can I help you?	**Kan jeg hjælpe Dem?**	kehn yigh **yehl**per dehm
Can you direct me to...?	**Kan De vise mig vejen til...?**	kehn dee **vēē**sser migh **vigh**ern til

Wanting...?

It is often too brusque in Danish to say "I want". Use the more polite:

I'd like...	**Jeg vil gerne ha'...**	yigh veel **gehr**ner hæ
We'd like...	**Vi vil gerne ha'...**	vee veel **gehr**ner hæ
What do you want?	**Hvad ønsker De?**	vahdh **urn**skerr dee
Give me...	**Giv mig...**	gee migh*

* See page 16.

Give it to me.	**Giv mig den.**	gee migh dehn
Give it to me.	**Giv mig det.**	gee migh day
Bring me...	**Bring mig...**	bring migh
Bring it to me.	**Bring mig den.**	bring migh dehn
Bring it to me.	**Bring mig det.**	bring migh day
Show me.	**Vis mig.**	vēēss migh
Show it to me.	**Vis mig den.**	vēēss migh dehn
Show it to me.	**Vis mig det.**	vēēss migh day
I'm hungry.	**Jeg er sulten.**	yigh ayr **soo**ltern
I'm thirsty.	**Jeg er tørstig.**	yigh ayr **turr**stee
I'm tired.	**Jeg er træt.**	yigh ayr treht
I'm lost.	**Jeg er faret vild.**	yigh ayr **faa**erd veel
I'm looking for...	**Jeg kigger efter...**	yigh **kigg**er **ehf**terr
It's important.	**Det er vigtigt.**	day ayr **vik**tee
It's urgent.	**Det haster.**	day **hahs**derr
Hurry up!	**Skynd Dem!**	skurn dehm

It is/There is...

It is...	**Den er...**	dehn ayr
It is...	**Det er...**	day ayr
Is it...?	**Er den...?**	ayr dehn
Is it...?	**Er det...?**	ayr day
It isn't...	**Den er ikke...**	dehn ayr **igg**er
It isn't...	**Det er ikke...**	day ayr **igg**er
Here it is.	**Her er den.**	hayr ayr dehn
Here it is.	**Her er det.**	hayr ayr day
Here they are.	**Her er de.**	hayr ayr dee
There it is.	**Der er den.**	dayr ayr dehn
There it is.	**Der er det.**	dayr ayr day
There they are	**Der er de.**	**dayr** ayr dee
There is/are...	**Der er...**	dayr ayr
Is there/are there...?	**Er der/Er der...?**	ayr **dayr**/ayr dayr
There isn't/aren't (any).	**Der er ikke (nogen).**	dayr ayr **igg**er **nōā**ern

Adjectives

big/small	stor/lille	stoar/**leeler**
quick/slow	hurtigt/langsomt	hoorteet/**lahng**somt
early/late	tidligt/sent	teedhleet/saynt
cheap/expensive	billig/dyr	beelee/dewr
near/far	nær/fjern	nær/fyehrn
hot/cold	varm/kold	vahrm/kol
full/empty	fuld/tom	fool/tom
easy/difficult	nemt/svært	nehmt/svær
heavy/light	tung/let	toong/leht
open/shut	åben/lukket	awbern/**looker**t
right/wrong	rigtig/forkert	riktee/forkayrt
old/new	gammel/ny	gahmerl/new
old/young	gammel/ung	gahmerl/oong
next/last	næste/sidste	nehster/**seester**
beautiful/ugly	smuk/grim	smook/grim
free (vacant)/occupied	ledigt/optaget	laydheet/optaiyert
good/bad	god/dårlig	goadh/**dawrlee**
better/worse	bedre/værre	behdhrer/vehrer

Quantities...

a little/a lot	lidt/meget	lit/**mighert**
much/many	meget/mange	mighert/**mahnger**
more/less	mere/mindre	mayrer/mindrer
enough/too much	nok/for meget	nok/foar mighert
some (any)	nogen	noaern

Prepositions

at	**ved**	vaydh
on	**på**	paw
in	**i**	ee
to	**til**	til
from	**fra**	fraa
inside	**indeni/indenfor**	innernēē/innernfor
outside	**udenfor**	ōōdhernfor
up/upstairs	**op/ovenpå**	op/o°°ernpaw
down/downstairs	**ned/nedenunder**	naydh/nāydhernnoonerr
after	**efter**	ehfterr
before	**før**	fūrr
with	**med**	maydh
without	**uden**	ōōdhern
through	**gennem**	gehnerm
toward(s)	**imod**	eemoadh
until	**indtil**	intil
during	**i løbet af**	ee lūrbert ah

...and a few more useful words

and	**og**	oa
or	**eller**	ehlerr
not	**ikke**	igger
nothing	**intet**	intert
none	**ingen**	ingern
very	**meget**	mighert
too (also)	**også**	ossaw
soon	**snart**	snahrt
perhaps	**måske**	moskay
here/there	**her/der**	hayr/dayr
now/then	**nu/da**	noo/daa

Arrival

You've arrived. Whether you've come by ship or plane, you'll have to go through passport and customs formalities. (For car/border control, see page 146.)

There's certain to be somebody around who speaks English. That's why we're making this a brief section. What you really want is to be off to your hotel in the shortest possible time. And here are the steps to get these formalities out of the way quickly.

Passport control

Here's my passport.	Her er mit pas.	hayr ayr meet pahss
I'll be staying...	Jeg bliver her...	yigh blēēerr hayr
a few days	et par dage	eht pahr daier
a week	en uge	ehn ōōer
two weeks	to uger	toa ōōerr
a month	en måned	ehn mawnerdh
I don't know yet.	Det ved jeg ikke endnu.	day vaydh yigh igger aynoo
I'm here on holiday.	Jeg er her på ferie.	yigh ayr hayr paw fehrēēer
I'm here on business.	Jeg er her på forretningsrejse.	yigh ayr hayr paw forraytneengsrighsser
I'm just passing through.	Jeg er kun på gennemrejse.	yigh ayr koon paw gehnermrighsser

If the going gets tough:

| I'm sorry, I don't understand. | Undskyld, jeg forstår Dem ikke. | oonskewl yigh forstawr dehm igger |
| Is there anyone here who speaks English? | Er her nogen, der taler engelsk? | ayr hayr nōāern dayr tailerr ehngerlsk |

Customs

For nationals of the United Kingdom and Eire, duty-free import allowances to Denmark vary slightly *depending on what country you're arriving from*. Residents of the U.S.A. and Canada, and in fact of any country outside Europe, fall into a separate category.

All figures given in the chart below are subject to change without notice.

from	Cigarettes		Cigars		Tobacco	Spirits		Dinner wine
EEC	300	or	75	or	400 g.	1½ l.	and	4 l.
Europe non-EEC	200	or	50	or	250 g.	1 l.	and	2 l.
outside Europe	400	or	100	or	500 g.	1 l.*	and	2 l.*

*Transiting via an EEC country: 1½ l. and 4 l.

I've nothing to declare.	**Jeg har intet at fortolde.**	yigh haar intert aht fortoaler
I've a...	**Jeg har...**	yigh haar
carton of cigarettes	**en karton cigaretter**	ehn kahrtoang siggahrayderr
bottle of whisky	**en flaske whisky**	ehn flahsker "whisky"
bottle of wine	**en flaske vin**	ehn flahsker veen
Must I pay on this?	**Skal jeg betale noget for dette?**	skahl yigh bertaaler noaert foar dehder
How much?	**Hvor meget?**	voar mighert
It's for my personal use.	**Det er til mit personlige forbrug.**	day ayr til meet payrsoanleeer forbroo
It's not new.	**Det er ikke nyt.**	day ayr igger newt

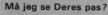

Må jeg se Deres pas?	Your passport, please.
Hår De noget at fortolde?	Have you anything to declare?
Vær venlig at åbne denne kuffert/taske.	Please open this suitcase/bag.
De skal betale told af dette.	You'll have to pay duty on this.
Har De mere bagage?	Have you any more luggage?

Baggage—Porters

Porters are few and far between, so best avail yourself of the free luggage trolleys.

Where are the luggage trolleys?	**Hvor er bagage-vognene?**	vōar ayr bah**gaash**er-**voan**erner
Porter!	**Drager!**	**dra**herr
That's mine.	**Det er min.**	day ayr mēēn
That's my...	**Det er min...**	day ayr mēēn
bag/luggage/suitcase	**taske/bagage/kuffert**	**tahs**ker/bah**gaash**err **koo**ffert
That...one.	**Den...dér.**	dehn...dayr
big/small	**store/lille**	**stoa**rer/**lee**ler
blue/brown	**blå/brune**	blaw/**brōō**ner
black/plaid	**sorte/skotskternede**	**soar**ter/**skoats**taynerdher
There's one piece missing.	**Der mangler én.**	dayr **mahng**lerr ehn
Take these bags to...	**Vær venlig at bringe disse tasker til...**	vær **vehn**lee aht **bring**er **dees**ser **tahs**kerr til
the bus	**bussen**	**boos**sern
the luggage lockers	**bagage boksene**	bah**gaash**er **boaks**erner
a taxi	**en taxi**	ehn **tahk**si
How much is that?	**Hvor meget bliver det?**	vōar **migh**ert **blēē**err day

FOR TIPPING, see page 1

Changing money

You'll find a bank at the Copenhagen airport and at most provincial airports too. If it's closed, don't worry. You'll be able to change money at your hotel.

In Copenhagen, the exchange office at the Central Railway Station stays open every day of the week from 7 a.m. to 10 p.m.

Full details about money and currency exchange are given on pages 134–136.

Where's the nearest currency exchange office?	**Hvor er det nær- meste vekselkontor?**	vōar ayr day **nærmerster** **vayks**erl**koantōar**
Can you change these traveller's cheques?	**Vil De indløse disse rejsechecks?**	veel dee inl**ū**rsser **deesser righsserchayks**
I want to change some...	**Jeg vil gerne veksle nogle...**	yigh veel **gehrner** **vayks**ler n**ōā**ler
dollars	**dollars**	**dollars**s
pounds	**pund**	poon
Can you change this into Danish crowns?	**Vil De veksle dette til danske kroner?**	veel dee **vayks**ler **deh**der til **dahns**ker kr**ōā**nerr
What's the exchange rate?	**Hvad er kursen?**	vahdh ayr **koors**sern

Directions

How do I get to...?	**Hvordan kommer jeg til...?**	vordahn **koame**rr yigh til
Where's the bus into town?	**Hvor er bussen til byen?**	vōar ayr **boos**sern til b**ēw**ern
Where can I get a taxi?	**Hvor kan jeg få fat i en taxi?**	vōar kehn yigh faw faht ee ehn **tah**ksi
Where can I rent a car?	**Hvor kan jeg leje en bil?**	vōar kehn yigh l**Igh**er ehn b**ēē**l

Hotel reservations

At Copenhagen main railway station you can make hotel reservations at the office marked *P*. Larger provincial towns offer similar facilities.

FOR NUMBERS, see page 175

ARRIVAL

Car rental

There are car rental firms at Kastrup and at most provincial airports and terminals and some member of the staff will usually speak English. However, if nobody does, try one of the following:

I'd like a...	**Jeg vil gerne leje en...**	yigh veel **gehr**ner **ligh**er ehn
car	**bil**	b**ēē**l
small car	**lille bil**	**leel**er b**ēē**l
large car	**stor bil**	stoar b**ēē**l
sports car	**sportsvogn**	**spoarts**voan
station-wagon	**stationcar**	"station-car"
I'd like it for...	**Jeg skal bruge den...**	yigh skahl br**ōō**er dehn
a day	**en dag**	ehn dai
4 days	**4 dage**	4 **dai**er
a week	**en uge**	ehn **ōō**er
2 weeks	**2 uger**	2 **ōō**err
What's the charge per...?	**Hvad koster det pr...?**	vahdh **koas**terr day pehr
day	**dag**	dai
week	**uge**	**ōō**er
Does that include mileage?	**Er det med kilometerpenge?**	ayr day maydh keeloam**āy**dherr**payn**ger
What's the charge per kilometre?	**Hvad koster det pr. kilometer?**	vahdh **koas**terr day pehr keeloam**āy**dherr
Is petrol (gasoline) included?	**Er benzinen iberegnet?**	ayr bayns**ēē**nern **ee**berrighnert
I want full insurance.	**Jeg ønsker fuld forsikring.**	yigh **urn**skerr fool forseek**reeng**
I'll be doing about 200 kilometres.	**Jeg skal køre circa 200 kilometer.**	yigh skahl k**ūr**rer **seer**kah 200 keeloam**āy**dherr
What's the deposit?	**Hvor meget skal der betales i depositum?**	v**ōā**r **migh**ert skahl dayr bertaalerss ee deh-**poass**eetoom
I've a credit card.	**Jeg har et kreditkort.**	yigh haar eht kray**deet**koart
Here's my driving licence.	**Her er mit kørekort.**	hayr ayr meet k**ūr**rerkoart

FOR SIGHTSEEING, see page 75

Note: In Denmark you can drive on your own licence; but check if an international licence is required for other countries you may visit.

Taxis

Cabs can be hailed in the street or ordered by phone. They are recognized by a *Taxi* or *Taxa* sign. You'll find taxi ranks at airports, railway stations and at various points in the cities. Meters are usually fitted to the dashboard of the taxi, showing the fare inclusive of tip. Rates may differ from place to place, it's usually best to ask the approximative fare beforehand.

Where can I get a taxi?	**Hvor kan jeg få en taxi?**	vōār kehn yigh faw ehn tahksi
Please get me a cab.	**Vil De skaffe mig en vogn?**	veel dee **skahf**er migh ehn voan
What's the fare to...?	**Hvad koster det til...?**	vahdh **koast**err day til
How far is it to...?	**Hvor langt er der til...?**	vōār lahngt ayr dayr til
Take me to...	**Kør mig til...**	kūrr migh til
this address	**denne adresse**	**dehn**er ahd**rayss**er
the town centre	**centrum**	**sayn**troom
the...Hotel	**Hotel...**	hoa**tayl**
Turn...at the next corner.	**Drej til...ved næste hjørne.**	drigh til...vaydh **nehs**ter y**ūr**rner
left	**venstre**	**vain**strer
right	**højre**	**hoi**rer
Go straight ahead.	**Kør ligeud.**	kūrr **lēē**er**ōō**dh
Stop here, please.	**Vær venlig at holde her.**	vær **vehn**lee aht **hoal**er hayr
I'm in a hurry.	**Jeg skal skynde mig.**	yigh skahl **skewn**er migh
Could you drive more slowly?	**Vær venlig at køre langsommere.**	vær **vehn**lee aht **kūr**rer **lahng**somerer
Could you help me to carry my bags?	**Kan De hjælpe mig med bagagen?**	kehn dee **yehl**per migh maydh bah**gaash**ern

ARRIVAL

FOR TIPPING, see page 1

Hotel—Other accommodation

Early reservation is essential in most tourist centres during the high season. If you arrive without a booking, look for the Room Reservation Service, at the office marked with a *P*, at the main railway station in Copenhagen or have a travel agency or the Danish automobile club make the necessary arrangements for you. You can, of course, go directly to a hotel.

In Denmark, hotels are not graded by stars as in some other countries, but normally the price level is a fair guide to the standard.

Kro (kroa)	Similar to a country inn in England; this can be modest or luxurious, and often extremely charming.
Motel (moatayl)	Motels are becoming more widespread in Denmark, with improving services. Lists of recommended motels are available from tourist information offices or automobile associations.
Pensionat (paynseeoanaht)	This is a boarding-house, and the price of the room usually includes full- or half-board.
Missionshotel (meesyoanshoatayl)	A modest establishment offering comfortable accommodation and good service at fair prices.
Sommerhus (soamerhōōs)	This "summer cottage" may be a bungalow, private house or apartment in a holiday region. Further information from local tourist offices.
KFUM [YMCA] **KFUK** [YWCA]	As in other countries, these establishments are known for moderate rates and cleanliness.
Vandrerhjem (vahndrehryaym)	This is a Youth Hostel. You must be in possession of a membership card which it's advisable to obtain from your own national Youth Hostels Association.

FOR CAMPING, see page 90

Another popular holiday arrangement is *ferie på landet* (**feh**-rēēer paw **lahn**ert)—farmhouse holidays. Farmers usually entertain one or two visiting families at a time, with board, lodging and farm life included in the price.

A variant provides a room or an apartment on a farm, where you do your own cooking and are otherwise self-sufficient.

Note: Smaller establishments do not accept travellers' cheques or credit cards.

In this section, we're mainly concerned with the smaller and medium-priced hotels and boarding houses. You'll have no language difficulties in the luxury and first-class hotels where most of the staff speak English.

In the next few pages we consider your requirements—step by step—from arrival to departure. You needn't read all of it; just turn to the situation that applies.

HOTEL

Checking in—Reception

My name is...	Mit navn er...	meet nown ayr
I've a reservation.	Jeg har reserveret.	yigh haar rayssehrv**ay**rert
We've reserved two rooms, a single and a double.	Vi har reserveret to værelser, et enkelt og et dobbelt.	vee haar rayssehrv**ay**rert toa v**ær**erlsserr eht **ehn**kerlt oa eht **doa**berlt
I wrote to you last month.	Jeg skrev til Dem i sidste måned.	yigh skrayv til dehm ee **sees**ter **maw**nerdh
Here's the confirmation.	Her er bekræftel-sen.	hayr ayr berk**ræf**terlssern
I'd like (a)...	Jeg vil gerne have...	yigh veel **gehr**ner hæ
single room	et enkeltværelse	eht **ehn**kerltvæ**rerls**ser
double room	et dobbeltværelse	eht **doa**berltvæ**rerls**ser
two single rooms	to enkeltværelser	toa **ehn**kerltvæ**rerls**serr
room	et værelse	eht v**ær**erlsser
with twin beds	med to senge	maydh toa **sayng**er
with a bath	med bad	maydh bahdh
with a shower	med brusebad	maydh br**ōō**sserbahdh
with a balcony	med balkon	maydh bahl**koang**
with a view	med udsigt	maydh **ōō**dhsigt

We'd like a room...	Vi vil gerne have et værelse...	vee veel **gehr**ner hæ eht **vær**erlsser
in the front	mod gaden	moadh **gaad**hern
at the back	bagud	bah**ōō**dh
facing the sea	ud mod havet	ōōdh moadh **howert**
facing the courtyard	mod gården	moadh **gawrern**
It must be quiet.	Det skal være roligt.	day skahl **vær**er **roaleet**
Is there...?	Er der...?	ayr dayr
air conditioning	klimaanlæg	**klēē**mahahnlehg
heating	varme	**vahrmer**
a radio/a television set in the room	radio/fjernsyn på værelset	**rah**deeoa/fy**ær**nsewn paw **vær**erlssert
a laundry service	vaskeri-service	vahskerree-sayr**vēē**sser
room service	servering på værelset	sayrv**āy**reeng paw **vær**erlssert
hot water	varmt vand	**vahrmt** vahn
running water	rindende vand	**reen**erner vahn
a private toilet	privat toilet	pree**vaht** toa**ee**layt

How much?

What's the price...?	Hvad koster det...?	vahdh **koasterr** day
per week	pr. uge	pehr **ōō**er
per night	pr. nat	pehr naht
for bed and breakfast	for overnatning og morgenmad	foar o°°ernahtning oa **mōā**ernmahdh
excluding meals	uden måltider	**ōō**dhern mawlt**ēē**dherr
for full board	med fuld pension	maydh fool pahng**syoan**
for half board	med halv pension	maydh hahl pahng**syoan**
Does that include...?	Er det med...?	ayr day maydh
breakfast	morgenmad	**mōā**ernmahdh
meals	måltider	mawlt**ēē**dherr
service	betjening	beht**yāy**neeng
tax	afgift	**owgeeft**
Is there any reduction for children?	Er der nogen reduktion for børn?	ayr dayr **nōā**ern raydook**syoan** foar burrn
Do you charge for the baby?	Koster det noget for babyen?	**koasterr** day **nōā**ert foar **baibewern**
That's too expensive.	Det er for dyrt.	day ayr foar dewrt
Haven't you anything cheaper?	Har De ikke noget, der er billigere?	haar dee **igger** **nōā**ert dayr ayr beel**ēēerrer**

FOR NUMBERS, see page 175

How long?

We'll be staying…	Vi bliver…	vee bl**ēē**err
overnight only	kun natten over	koon **nah**tern o°°err
a few days	et par dage	eht pahr **dai**er
a week (at least)	(mindst) en uge	(meenst) ehn **ōō**er
I don't know yet.	Det ved jeg ikke endnu.	day vaydh yigh **igg**er **ay**noo

Decision

May I see the room?	Må jeg se værelset?	maw yigh s**āy vǣ**rerlssert
No, I don't like it.	Nej, det synes jeg ikke om.	nigh day s**ēw**nerss yigh **igg**er oam
It's too…	Det er for…	day ayr foar
cold	koldt	kolt
hot	varmt	**vah**rmt
dark	mørkt	**mu**rrkt
small	lille	**lee**ler
noisy	støjende	**stoi**erner
I asked for a room with a bath.	Jeg bad om et værelse med bad.	yigh bahdh oam eht **vǣ**rerlsser maydh bahdh
Do you have anything…?	Har De et…?	haar dee eht
better	bedre	**bay**dhrer
bigger	større	**stu**rrer
cheaper	billigere	**beel**ēēerrer
quieter	roligere	**roal**ēēerrer
higher up	højere oppe	**hoi**errer **oa**ber
lower down	længere nede	**lain**gerrer n**āy**dher
Do you have a room with a better view?	Har De et værelse med bedre udsigt?	haar dee eht **vǣ**rerlsser maydh **bay**dhrer **ōō**dhsigt
That's fine. I'll take it.	Det er i orden. Det tager jeg.	day ayr ee **oa**rdern. day taar yigh

Bills

These are usually paid weekly or upon departure if your stay is shorter. Most hotels offer a reduction for children; some don't charge at all.

FOR DAYS OF THE WEEK, see page 181

Tipping

Not a big problem since basically you don't give tips. Hotel and restaurant bills always include service; tip only if special services have been rendered.

Registration

Upon arrival at a hotel or boarding-house you'll be asked to fill in a registration form (*tilmeldelsesblanket*—**til**maylerlsserssblan**kayt**). It asks your name, home address, passport number and further destination. It's almost certain to carry an English translation. If it doesn't, ask the desk-clerk (*portieren*—poar**tyeh**ern):

What does this mean?   **Hvad betyder dette?**   vahdh bert$\overline{ew}$dherr dehder

The desk-clerk will probably ask you for your passport. He may want to keep it for a while, even overnight. Don't worry. You'll get it back. He may want to ask you the following questions:

Må jeg se Deres pas?	May I see your passport?
Vil De være så venlig at udfylde denne tilmeldelsesblanket?	Would you mind filling in this registration form?
Vil De skrive under her?	Please sign here.
Hvor længe bliver De?	How long will you be staying?

What's my room number?	**Hvilket nummer har mit værelse?**	vilkert **noommerr** haar meet **væ**rerlsser
Will you have our bags sent up?	**Vil De sende bagagen op?**	veel dee **sayner** bah**gaash**ern op

FOR TIPPING, see page 1

Service, please

bellboy	piccolo	peekoaloa
maid	stuepige	st $\overline{oo}$erp$\overline{ee}$er
manager	direktør	diraykturr
room service	etagetjener	ehtaashertyāynerr
switchboard operator	omstillingsdame	oamstilingsdaamer
waiter	tjener	tyāynerr
waitress	servitrice	sayrveetr$\overline{ee}$sser

Address the waiter as *tjener* (**tyāyn**nerr) and the waitress as *frøken* (**frūr**gern).

General requirements

Please ask the maid to come up.	**Vær så venlig at bede stuepigen komme op.**	vær saw vehnlee aht bay st$\overline{oo}$erp$\overline{ee}$ern koamer op
Who is it?	**Hvem er det?**	vehm ayr day
Just a minute.	**Lige et øjeblik.**	l$\overline{ee}$er eht oierblik
Come in!	**Kom ind!**	koam in
Is there a bath on this floor?	**Er der et bade-værelse på denne etage?**	ayr dayr eht baadher-værerlsser paw dehner ehtaasher
Where's the plug for the razor?	**Hvor er stikket til barbermaskinen?**	v$\overline{oa}$r ayr stiggert til bahrbāyrmahsk$\overline{ee}$nern
What's the voltage here?	**Hvad er spæn-dingen?**	vahdh ayr spaineengern
Can we have breakfast in our room?	**Kan vi få morgen-mad på værelset?**	kehn vee faw m$\overline{oa}$ern-mahdh paw værerlssert
I'd like to leave these in your safe.	**Jeg vil gerne opbe-vare disse i Deres pengeskab.**	yigh veel gehrner ophervaarer deesser ee dayrerss payngerskahb
Can you find me a baby-sitter?	**Kan De finde en baby-sitter?**	kehn dee finner ehn "baby-sitter"

BETJENING—RING HER
RING FOR SERVICE

HOTEL SERVICE

May I have a/an/some...?	Kan jeg få...?	kehn yigh faw
ashtray	et askebæger	eht **ahs**kerbaierr
bath towel	et badehåndklæde	eht **baadh**erhawnklaidher
extra blanket	et ekstra tæppe	eht **ayk**strah **teh**ber
envelopes	nogle konvolutter	n**ōā**ler koanvolo**odd**err
(more) hangers	(flere) bøjler	(**flay**rer) **boi**lerr
ice cubes	nogle isterninger	n**ōā**ler **ēēs**st**āy**rneengerr
pillow	en hovedpude	ehn ho**°°**erdhp**ōō**dher
reading lamp	en læselampe	ehn **laiss**erlahmper
soap	et stykke sæbe	eht **stewg**ger **sai**ber
writing paper	noget skrivepapir	n**ōā**ert skr**ēē**verpahp**ēē**r
Where's the...?	Hvor er...?	v**ōā**r ayr
bathroom	badeværelset	**baadh**erv**ā**rerlssert
beauty salon	skønhedssalonen	sk**urn**haydhssahlongern
dining-room	spisesalen	sp**ēē**ssersaalern
hairdresser's	frisøren	frees**ūr**rern
television room	fjernsynsstuen	fy**ā**rnsewnsst**ōō**ern
toilet	toilettet	toaee**layd**ert

Breakfast

Breakfast (*morgenmad*—m**ōā**ernmahdh) in a Danish hotel is a far cry from the Spartan "continental breakfast" of a bread roll and a cup of coffee. Bread rolls, meat, cheese, jam, pastries and possibly an egg are accompanied by a glass of milk or fruit juice, followed by tea or coffee. A distinctive breakfast pastry, light and flaky, is *wienerbrød* (v**ēē**nerbrurdh).

I'll have a/an/some...	Jeg vil gerne have...	yigh veel **gehr**ner hæ
bacon and eggs	bacon og æg	"bacon" oa ehg
cereals:		
cold	cornflakes	"cornflakes"
hot	havregrød	**howr**ergrurdh
eggs	æg	ehg
boiled egg	kogt æg	koat ehg
soft/medium/hard	blød/mellem/hård	blurdh/**may**lerm/hawr
fried eggs	spejlæg	**spigh**lehg
scrambled eggs	røræg	r**ūr**rehg

fruit juice	**frugtsaft**	froogtsahft
grapefruit	**grapefrugt**	"grape"-froogt
orange	**appelsin**	ahberls **ēēn**
pineapple/tomato	**ananas/tomat**	ahnahnahss/toamaat
ham and eggs	**skinke og æg**	skeenker oa ehg
jam	**syltetøj**	sewltertoi
marmalade	**orangemarmelade**	oarahnshermahrmerlaadher
omelet	**en omelet**	ehn oamerleht
pancakes	**pandekager**	pahnerkaaerr
porridge	**havregrød**	howrergrurdh
sausages	**pølser**	purlsserr
toast	**ristet brød**	reestert brurdh
yoghurt	**yoghurt**	yoghoort
May I have some…?	**Kan jeg få…?**	kehn yigh faw
hot/cold milk	**varm/kold mælk**	vahrm/kol mehlk
cream/sugar	**fløde/sukker**	flūrdher/**sooggerr**
bread/rolls	**brød/rund-**	brurdh/**roon-**
	stykker	stewggerr
butter	**smør**	smurr
salt/pepper	**salt/peber**	sahlt/**peh°°err**
coffee/tea	**kaffe/te**	kahfer/teh
hot chocolate	**varm chokolade**	vahrm shoakoalaadher
lemon/honey	**citron/honning**	seetr**ōān**/**hoa**neeng
hot water	**varmt vand**	vahrmt vahn
Could you bring me a…?	**Vil De bringe mig…?**	veel dee **breeng**er migh
glass/cup	**et glas/en kop**	eht glahss/ehn koap
knife/fork	**en kniv/en gaffel**	ehn kn**ēē**v/ehn **gah**ferl
napkin	**en serviet**	ehn sayrv**ēē**eht
plate	**en tallerken**	ehn tahl**āy**rkern
serviette	**en serviet**	ehn sayrv**ēē**eht
spoon	**en ske**	ehn skeh

HOTEL SERVICE

Difficulties

The…doesn't work.	**…virker ikke.**	v**ee**rkerr **ig**ger
air-conditioner	**klimaanlægget**	kl**ēē**mahahnlehggert
fan	**viften**	v**ee**ftern
heating	**radiatoren**	rahdeeahtoarern
light	**lyset**	lewssert
radio	**radioen**	**rah**deeoaern
tap	**vandhanen**	**vahn**haanern
toilet	**toilettet**	toaeelaydert
ventilator	**ventilatoren**	vaynteelahtoarern

FOR EATING OUT, see pages 38–64

The wash-basin is clogged.	**Håndvasken er tilstoppet.**	**hawn**vahskern ayr **til**stobbert
The window is jammed.	**Vinduet binder.**	veend$\overline{oo}$ert beenerr
The blind is stuck.	**Persiennen sidder fast.**	pehrs$\overline{ee}$ehnern saydherr fahst
I can't open the wardrobe.	**Jeg kan ikke åbne klædeskabet.**	yigh kehn **i**gger **awb**ner **klaid**herskahbert
The door won't lock.	**Døren kan ikke låses.**	**dur**rern kehn **i**gger **laws**serss
These aren't my shoes.	**Det er ikke mine sko.**	day ayr **i**gger m$\overline{ee}$ner skoa
This isn't my laundry.	**Det er ikke mit vasketøj.**	day ayr **i**gger meet **vahs**kertoi
There's no hot water.	**Der er ikke noget varmt vand.**	dayr ayr **i**gger n$\overline{oa}$ert vahrmt vahn
I've left my key in my room.	**Jeg har glemt nøglen på værelset.**	yigh haar glaymt noilern paw **vær**erlssert
The bulb is burnt out.	**Pæren er sprunget.**	**pær**ern ayr **sproong**ert
The...is broken.	**...er i stykker.**	ayr ee **stew**ggerr
lamp	**lampen**	**lahm**pern
plug	**stikket**	**stig**gert
shutter	**skodden**	**skoad**hern
switch	**kontakten**	**koan**tahktern
venetian blind	**persiennen**	pehrs$\overline{ee}$ehnern
window shade	**rullegardinet**	**rool**ergahrd$\overline{ee}$nert
Can you get it repaired?	**Kan De få det repareret?**	kehn de faw day raypahr$\overline{ay}$rert

Telephone—Mail—Callers

Can you get me 68-34-29 in Copenhagen?	**Vil de give mig 68 34 29 i København?**	veel dee gee migh 68-34-29 ee kurbern**hown**
Has anyone telephoned me?	**Har nogen ringet til mig?**	haar n$\overline{oa}$ern reengert til migh
Do you have any stamps?	**Sælger De frimærker?**	**sehl**gerr dee **free**mærkerr
Would you please mail this for me?	**Vil De være venlig at sende dette for mig?**	veel dee **vær**er **vehn**lee aht **say**ner **deh**der foar migh
Are there any messages for me?	**Er der nogen besked til mig?**	ayr dayr n$\overline{oa}$ern beh**skehdh** til migh

FOR POST OFFICE AND TELEPHONE, see page 137–141

Checking out

May I please have my bill?	Må jeg bede om regningen?	maw yigh bay oam **righ**-neengern
I'm leaving early tomorrow.	Jeg rejser tidligt i morgen.	yigh **righ**sserr **teedh**leet ee **mōā**ern
Please have my bill ready.	Vil De gøre min regning klar?	veel dee **gūr**rer m**ēē**n **righ**neeng klahr
We'll be checking out soon/around noon.	Vi rejser snart/ ved middagstid.	vee **righ**sserr snahrt/ vaydh **mid**aisteedh
When is check-out time?	Hvad tid skal man afgive værelset?	vahdh teedh skahl mahn owgee v**ǣ**rerlssert
I must leave at once.	Jeg er nødt til at rejse straks.	yigh ayr nurdh til aht **righ**sser strahks
Is everything included?	Er alt iberegnet?	ayr ahlt **ee**berrighnert
You've made a mistake in this bill, I think.	Jeg tror, der er en fejl på regningen.	yigh troar dayr ayr ehn fighl paw **righ**neengern
Can you get us a taxi?	Vil De skaffe os en taxi?	veel dee **skah**fer oss ehn **tah**ksi
When's the next... to Copenhagen?	Hvornår afgår næste ...til København?	vornawr owgawr **neh**ster ...til kurbern**hown**
boat	skib	sk**ēē**b
bus	bus	booss
plane	fly	flew
train	tog	toa
Would you send someone to bring down our baggage?	Kan vi få bagagen bragt ned?	kehn vee faw bah**gaas**hern braht naydh
We're in a great hurry.	Vi har meget travlt.	vee haar **migh**ert trowlt
Here's the forwarding address.	Her er min næste adresse.	hayr ayr m**ēē**n **neh**ster ah**drayss**er
You have my home address.	De har min faste adresse.	dee haar m**ēē**n **fah**ster ah**drayss**er
It's been a very enjoyable stay.	Det har været et meget behageligt ophold.	day haar v**ǣ**rert eht **migh**ert berh**aaer**leet **op**hoal
I hope we'll come again sometime.	Jeg håber, vi kom-mer igen engang.	yigh **haw**berr vee **koam**err eeg**gayn** ehng**ahng**

HOTEL SERVICE

FOR TAXI, see page 27

Eating out

There are many types of places where you can eat and drink in Denmark:

Bar—Pub— Diskotek (bahr— purb— deeskoat**ayk**)	For drinks and cold meals almost round the clock (closed only between 2 and 5 in the morning!) Many bars come up with imaginative decors from naval interiors to futuristic 2000 A.D. motifs. The discotheques and most pubs are youth-oriented, in dancing music and noise levels.
Bodega— Værtshus (bod**ay**gah værtsh**oo**ss)	A more attractive and relaxed form of snackbar, these establishments serve drinks and a choice of perhaps a dozen simple meals. They have grown in popularity recently and you'll find them even in smaller towns.
Café (kahf**ay**)	Unlike its French namesake, generally serves drinks only.
Cafeteria (kahfert**ay**reeah)	Food and drinks, often on a self-service basis. You will find cafeterias in department stores and large supermarkets. Hard liquor may not be served, but beer is generally available.
Kaffebar (**kah**ferbahr)	Mainly light snacks in this close equivalent of a transport café or diner. This is generally a place where young people meet—because it's cheap and convivial. Liquor is rarely served, but coffee flows freely, of course.
Pølsevogn (**purl**sservoan)	A street stand selling hot-dogs.

Konditori (koandeetoaree)	Pastry shops often serve coffee, tea or even a rich ice-cream dessert. If your's is a sweet tooth, this is the place to sample the best of Danish pastry during morning or afternoon tea or coffee break.
Kro (kroa)	A country inn, serving drinks and full meals, having often their own *kroplatte* (**kroa**plahder) as a speciality. Many are charming and romantically rustic—but, usually, the more attractive the décor the higher the prices! The cooking can be worth it nevertheless.
Restaurant (raystoarahng)	The major cities offer a large choice of restaurants serving Danish specialities. Study the menu displayed outside the entrance. It will list the daily special *dagens ret* (**dai**ernss rayt), as well as à-la-carte items.

Meal times and eating habits

We assume that you've had breakfast at your hotel. See page 34 for a breakfast menu.

Lunch (*frokost*–**froa**koast) is generally served from noon until 2 p.m.

Dinner (*aftensmad*—**ahf**ternsmahdh) time is flexible. The Danes normally have their evening meal between 6 and 8 p.m., but restaurants in all large towns serve food until late at night. In addition to à-la-carte items, one or more set menus may be listed.

Denmark is known as *Nordens spisekammer,* the larder of the North, with its vast farmland, which has yielded abundant produce for centuries. Don't turn down an invitation for a "cup of coffee" in the country: it will probably be served on a large table filled with exquisite homemade pas-

EATING OUT

tries. Another eye-opener will await you if you are invited to a copious Danish *koldt bord* (see page 48).

Lunch is a secondary, often cold meal—but hardly light. It might consist of *smørrebrød* (**smurr**erbrurdh) (filling open-faced sandwiches—see page 45) with a glass of milk or beer. Alternatively, lunch might call for *en platte* (ehn **plahd**er), a cold plate made up of six to eight Danish specialities—such as herring, fish fillet, liver paste, ham, Danish salami, possibly a rissole, a slice of beef, and cheese, all eaten with bread and butter.

Dinner, consisting of two or three substantial courses, is the main meal of the day. Soup or a cold fish dish is followed by a main course of meat, vegetables, and, inevitably, potatoes; then ice cream, doughnuts, cheese, or some *rødgrød* (**rurd**-grurdh), a soft fruit jelly.

Many restaurants serve both Danish dishes and international cuisine. All over the country—sometimes on small islands or even in remote towns—you'll find Chinese and Japanese restaurants.

Hvad ønsker De?	What would you like?
Jeg anbefaler dette.	I recommend this.
Hvad ønsker De at drikke?	What would you like to drink?
Vi har ikke...	We haven't got...
Ønsker De...?	Do you want...?

Value-added tax and service charge are automatically added to your bill. Danes are not tip-minded, though after a meal out you may want to round off with an extra krone or two for good service.

Hungry

I'm hungry/ I'm thirsty.	**Jeg er sulten/ Jeg er tørstig.**	yigh ayr **sōōltern/** yigh ayr **turrstee**
Can you recommend a good restaurant?	**Kan De anbefale mig en god restaurant?**	kehn dee **ahn**berfaaler migh ehn goadh raystoa- **rahng**
Are there any good, cheap restaurants around here?	**Er der en god og billig restaurant her i nærheden?**	ayr dayr ehn goadh oa **bee**lee raystoa**rahng** hayr ee n**ǣr**rehhdhern

If you want to be sure of getting a table in a well-known restaurant, it may be better to telephone in advance.

I'd like to reserve a table for 4.	**Jeg vil gerne reser- vere et bord til 4.**	yigh veel **gehr**ner ray- sseehrv**ǟy**rer eht boar til 4
We'll come at 8.	**Vi kommer kl. 8.**	vee **koa**merr kloa**gg**ern 8

Asking and ordering

Good evening. I'd like a table for 3.	**God aften. Jeg vil gerne have et bord til 3.**	goadh **ahf**tern. yigh veel **gehr**ner hæ eht boar til 3.
Could we have a table...?	**Kan vi få et bord...?**	kehn vee faw eht boar
in the corner by the window outside on the terrace	**i hjørnet ved vinduet udenfor på terrassen**	ee y**ūr**rnet vaydh **veend**ōōert **ōō**dhernfoar paw tayr**rah**sern
May I please have the menu?	**Må jeg bede om spisekortet?**	maw yigh bay oam sp**ēēss**erkoartert
What's this?	**Hvad er dette?**	vahdh ayr **deh**der
Do you have...?	**Er der...?**	ayr dayr
a set menu local dishes a children's menu	**en dagens ret lokale retter en ret for børn**	ehn **dai**erns rayt **loa**kaaler **ray**derr ehn rayt foar burrn
I'd like...	**Jeg vil gerne have...**	yigh veel **gehr**ner hæ
Is service included?	**Er betjening ibe- regnet?**	ayr beht**yǟy**neeng **ee**eber- righnert

Could we have (a/an)...?	Kan vi få...?	kehn vee faw
ashtray	et askebæger	eht ahskerbaierr
fork	en gaffel	ehn gahferl
glass	et glas	eht glahss
knife	en kniv	ehn knēēv
napkin	en serviet	ehn sayrvēēeht
plate	en tallerken	ehn tahlāyrkern
spoon	en ske	ehn skeh

I'd like a/an/some...	Jeg vil gerne have...	yigh veel gehrner hæ
appetizer	en forret	ehn foarrayt
beer	en øl	ehn url
bread	noget brød	nōāert brurdh
butter	noget smør	nōāert smurr
cabbage	kål	kawl
cheese	noget ost	nōāert oast
chips	pommes frites	pomfrit
dessert	en dessert	ehn dehssayrt
fish	fisk	feesk
french fries	pommes frites	pomfrit
fruit	noget frugt	nōāert froogt
game	en vildt-anretning	ehn veeltahnraytneeng
ice-cream	en is-anretning	ehn ēēssahnraytneeng
lemon	citron	seetrōān
lettuce	grøn salat	grurn sahlaat
meat	kød	kurdh
milk	mælk	mehlk
mustard	sennep	sehnerp
noodles	nudler	noodhlerr
oil	olie	oalyer
pepper	peber	peh°°err
potatoes	kartofler	kahrtoaflerr
rice	ris	rēēss
rolls	rundstykker	roonstewggerr
salad	salat	sahlaat
salt	salt	sahlt
seafood	en fiskeret	ehn feeskerrayt
soup	en suppe	ehn sooberr
sugar	noget sukker	nōāert sooggerr
tea	te	teh
vegetables	grønsager	grurnsaaerr
vinegar	eddike	ehdheegger
(iced) water	(is)vand	(ēēss)vahn
wine	vin	vēēn

FOR COMPLAINTS, see page 60

What's on the menu?

Our menu is presented according to courses. Under the headings below you'll find alphabetical lists of dishes that might be offered on a Danish menu with their English equivalents. You can also show the book to the waiter. If you want some fruit, for instance, show him the appropriate list and let him point to what's available. Use pages 41 and 42 for ordering in general.

Here then is our guide to good eating and drinking. Turn to the section you want.

EATING OUT

As many dishes are prepared to order, allow time for a main meal. The waiters don't expect you to rush.

Obviously, you aren't going to go through every course. If you've had enough, say:

Nothing more, thanks. **Ikke mere, tak.**　　　igger māȳrer tæk

Appetizers

When you are out eating in a Danish home, it is customary to thank the hostess for the meal by saying, *Tak for mad* (tæk foar mahdh), to which she will reply, *Velbekomme* (vaylber**koam**er), i.e. I hope you enjoyed the meal.

When ordering à-la-carte, Danes generally begin with one of the many tasty starters, whereas set menus often include none.

I'd like an appetizer.	**Jeg vil gerne have en forret.**	yigh veel **gehr**ner hæ ehn **foar**rayt
What do you recommend?	**Hvad kan De anbe-fale?**	vahdh kehn dee **ahn**berfaaler
agurk	ah**goork**	cucumbers
ansjoser	ahn**shōāss**err	anchovies
artiskokker	ahr**teeskoagg**err	artichokes
aspargeshoveder	ah**spahrsho°°erd**herr	asparagus tips
blandet hors d'oeuvre	**blah**nert "hors d'œuvre"	assorted appetizers
bøftartar	**burf**tahtahr	beef tartare
champignons	shahm**peeny**oan	mushrooms
frugtsaft	**froogt**sahft	fruit juice
ananas	**ah**nahnahss	pineapple
appelsin	ahberl**sēēn**	orange
grapefrugt	"grape"-froogt	grapefruit
tomat	toa**maat**	tomato
gåselever	**gaw**sserleh°°err	goose liver
hummer	**hoomm**err	lobster
kaviar	**kah**veeahr	caviar
krabbekød	**krah**berkurdh	crab
laks	lahks	salmon
røget	**roi**ert	smoked
gravet	**graa**vert	cured
makrel	mah**krayl**	mackerel
marineret	mahree**nāyr**ert	marinated
muslinger	**moos**leengerr	clams
oliven (fyldte)	oa**lēē**vern (**fewl**ter)	olives (stuffed)
radiser	rah**dēēss**err	radishes
rejer	**righ**err	shrimps
rogn	roan	roe
spegepølse	**spigh**erpurlsser	salami
salat	sah**laat**	salad
sardiner	sahr**dēēn**err	sardines

sild	seel	herring
røget	roiert	smoked
i lage	ee laagger	soused
marineret	mahreena̅y̅rert	marinated
skinke	skeenker	ham
tunfisk	to̅o̅nfeesk	tunny (US tuna)
vandmelon	vahnmehloan	watermelon
æg	ehg	egg
hårdkogt	hawrkoat	hard-boiled
østers	ursters	oysters
ål	awl	eel
i gelé	ee shehla̅y̅	jellied
røget	roiert	smoked

Smørrebrød

Smørrebrød (**smurr**erbrurdh) literally means "buttered bread". But what an understatement! Essentially, *smørrebrød* is a large buttered open-faced sandwich generously covered with one of a variety of delicacies: veal, beef tartare, fried liver, liver paste, salmon, smoked eel, cod-roe, caviar, shrimp, herring, ham, roast beef, salad or cheese. This main layer is garnished with a variety of accessories carefully selected to emphasize taste and appearance. The entire two-story high *smørrebrød* presented to you tastes as delightful as it looks.

Larger restaurants have a menu of *smørrebrød* items, often with an English translation. All you have to do is to tick off each item you want, giving your choice of bread too: *hvedebrød* (**vehdh**erbrurdh—wholemeal or wholewheat), *rugbrød* (**roo**brurdh—rye), *pumpernikkel-brød* (**poom**perrniggerl-brurdh—black bread).

Smørrebrød can be ordered from a delicatessen or in a restaurant at any time. They may be rather filling, so order one at a time. There are special *smørrebrød* for children.

If *smørrebrød* is to be the first course of a full-course meal, it's often accompanied by *snaps* (snahpss) (see page 62).

Salads

What salads do you have?	**Hvad slags salater har De?**	vahdh slahgss sahlaaderr haar dee

Chances are you'll find at least the following ones available:

agurksalat (ah**goork**sahlaat)	cucumber in a vinegar dressing
kyllingesalat (**kew**leengersahlaat)	chicken meat, macaroni, tomato slices, green peppers, olives, green peas, lettuce and mushrooms, covered with a tomato dressing
rødbeder (**rurdh**behdherr)	beetroot and diced apples in a mild dressing, possibly with horseradish
sellerisalat (**sehl**erreessahlaat)	celery salad with a cheese dressing or mayonnaise

The following preparations, though styled "salads" are mainly eaten on *smørrebrød* or as appetizers

italiensk salat (eetaalee**āÿnsk** sah**laat**)	diced carrots and asparagus, green peas, macaroni, mayonnaise
makrelsalat (mah**krayl**sahlaat)	mackerel (not always smoked) in tomato sauce topped with mayonnaise
rejesalat (**righ**ersahlaat)	shrimp, apple and celery, sometimes mixed with a tomato dressing, sometimes with a mayonnaise dressing
sildesalat (**seel**ersahlaat)	marinated or pickled herring, beetroot, apple and pickles in a spicy dressing

Egg dishes

The Danes are very fond of eggs. Omelets, offered in great variety also include the rather unusual *dessert-omelet* (deh-**ssayrt**oamerleht) with jam.

I'd like bacon and eggs.	**Jeg vil gerne have bacon og æg.**	yigh veel **gehr**ner hæ "bacon" oa ehg
et kogt æg **blødkogt/smilende/** **hårdkogt** **pocheret**	eht koat ehg **blurdh**koat/sm**ēē**lerner/ **hawr**koat poash**āÿ**rert	a boiled egg soft/medium/ hard poached

en omelet	ehn oamerleht	an omelet
med champignons	maydh **shahm**peenyoan	mushroom
med ost	maydh oast	cheese
med skinke	maydh **skeen**ker	ham
med tomater	maydh too**maa**derr	tomato
med kyllingelever	maydh **kew**leenger-lehᵒᵒerr	chicken-liver
med sukker og syltetøj	maydh **soog**gerr oa **sewl**tertoi	sugar and jam
røræg	rūᵣrehg	scrambled eggs
spejlæg	**spigh**lehg	fried eggs

Two egg specialities of Denmark are:

æggekage (**ehg**erkaaer)	"egg cake": scrambled eggs with onions, chives, potatoes and bacon bits
skidne æg (skēēdhner ehg)	poached or hard boiled eggs in a cream sauce, spiced with fish mustard and served with rye bread, decorated with diced bacon and chives

Soups

I'd like some soup.	**Jeg vil gerne have en suppe.**	yigh veel **gehr**ner hæ ehn **soob**ber
aspargessuppe	ah**spahrs**soobber	asparagus soup
champignonsuppe	**shahm**peenyoansoobber	mushroom soup
gule ærter	**gōō**ler ærterr	split-pea soup with salt pork
hummersuppe	**hoom**merrsoobber	lobster chowder
hønsekødsuppe	**hurns**serkurdhsoobber	chicken vegetables soup
klar suppe med boller og grønsager	klahr **soob**ber maydh **boa**lerr oa **grurn**saaerr	vegetable soup with meatballs
æblesuppe	**ehb**lersoobber	apple soup
ægte skildpaddesuppe	**ehg**ter **skeel**paadhersoobber	turtle soup

While on the subject of soups, here are two more which deserve mention more as main dishes. They are, in fact, country stews:

labskovs (**lahb**skoᵒᵒss)	beef, diced potatoes, slices of carrots and onions; served with rye bread
øllebrød (**ur**lerbrurdh)	rye bread cooked with Danish beer (hvidtøl), sugar and lemon, served with milk and cream

For an unusual kind of soup, you might like to try one of the following, which may also be served as dessert:

frugtsuppe (**froogt**soobber)	"fruit soup"; composed of a variety of dried fruits (often apricots and prunes): may be served chilled or hot
kråsesuppe (**krawss**ersoobber)	much the same as the above, but with the addition of chicken giblets and often apples

Koldt bord

In Sweden it's called *smörgåsbord*, the name by which this delightful Scandinavian institution is best known throughout the world. The same type of cold buffet is known as *koldt bord* (kolt boar) in Denmark.

In olden days this enormous buffet was common in homes as well as restaurants. Now home buffets are modest and you'll rarely come across a tremendous choice of dishes except in the larger restaurants.

You start at one end of the table, with herring, seafood, salads, and other titbits, and return as many times as you like.

In addition to fish and seafood there's certain to be a good selection of cold cuts, meat, liver paste and ham. Sometimes you cut your own slices fresh off the joint.

Despite its name, a *koldt bord* always includes a few hot items—meat balls, pork sausages, soup, fried potatoes etc. Several kinds of bread and butter are provided.

In private homes, the variety may be reduced but never the efforts to create special effects in the composition of the items and the table decoration.

Akvavit (see page 62) and beer go especially well with all this.

The whole ceremony is an experience which may last up to three hours. The price is the same however much you eat.

Fish and seafood

In Denmark, fresh fish is readily available everywhere. You can often watch the catch being brought in and, if you're cooking your own meals, buy in your provisions from the fresh-fish markets.

Don't miss the salmon. As for shrimp, you can't avoid them—they're an essential feature of *smørrebrød* (see page 45).

See the following page for some Danish fish specialities.

I'd like some fish.	**Jeg vil gerne have en fiskeret.**	yigh veel **gehrner** hæ ehn **feeskerrayt**
What kinds of seafood do you have?	**Hvad slags fisk har De?**	vahdh slahgss feesk haar dee
aborre	ahboarer	perch
ansjoser	ahnshoasserr	anchovies
blåmuslinger	blawmoosleengerr	mussels
forel	foarayl	trout
gedde	gehdher	pike
helleflynder	haylerflewnerr	halibut
hummer	hoommerr	lobster
karpe	kahrper	carp
klipfisk	kleepfeesk	salt cod
krabbe	krahber	crab
krebs	kraybss	crayfish
laks	lahks	salmon
makrel	mahkrayl	mackerel
pigvarre	pigvahrer	turbot
rejer	righerr	shrimp
rødspætte	rurspaider	plaice
røget sild	roiert seel	kipper
rogn	roan	roe
sardiner	sahrdeenerr	sardines
sild	seel	herring
skrubbe	skroobber	flounder
store rejer	stoarer righerr	prawns
søtunge	surtoonger	sole
stør	sturr	sturgeon
torsk	toarsk	cod
tunfisk	toonfeesk	tunny (US tuna)
ål	awl	eel
ørred	urrerdh	trout
østers	ursterss	oysters

There are many ways of preparing fish. Here is how you may want it served:

baked	**stegt i ovn**	staigt ee o°°n
cured	**gravet**	**graa**vert
fried	**stegt i panden**	staigt ee **pah**nern
grilled	**grilleret**	grily$\overline{ay}$rert
marinated	**marineret**	maareen$\overline{ay}$rert
poached	**pocheret**	poash$\overline{ay}$rert
sautéed	**brunet i smør**	br$\overline{oo}$nert ee smurr
smoked	**røget**	**roi**ert
steamed	**dampkogt**	**dahm**koat

Seafood specialities

blå foreller
(blaw foa**ray**lerr)

poached trout, served with boiled potatoes, melted butter, horseradish and lemon

vinkogt laks med pikant sovs
(v$\overline{ee}$nkoat lahks maydh pee**kahnt** so°°ss)

salmon poached in white wine, dressed with a spicy sauce and served with salad and potatoes

sild i karry
(seel ee **kaa**ree)

herring with curry sauce, served with rice, leeks and dark bread

sild, røget
(seel **roi**ert)

smoked herring on dark rye bread, garnished with a raw egg yolk, radishes and chives

rødspætte, stegt
(**rur**spaider staigt)

fried plaice served with boiled potatoes and either a parsley sauce or a mustard and herb cream dressing

torsk, kogt
(toarsk koat)

poached cod served with boiled potatoes and a mustard sauce

torskerogn, ristet
(**toars**kerroan **ree**stert)

fried cod-roe, cold or warm, served with a mustard and herb cream dressing or potato salad

ålesuppe
(**awl**ersoobber)

sweet-and-sour eel soup, with apples and prunes, served with dark rye bread

ål, stegt med stuvede kartofler
(awl staigt maydh st$\overline{oo}$overdher kahr**toaf**lerr)

fried eel with diced potatoes in a white sauce

Meat

Danish bacon and ham are world famous, and pork is in fact the Danes' favourite meat. In the past generation, the emphasis has been on lean pork, which you are sure to enjoy. But you'll have no difficulty getting beef or lamb in restaurants.

I'd like some...	Jeg vil gerne have noget...	yigh veel **gehr**ner hæ **n**o͞**a**ert
beef/lamb	**oksekød/lammekød**	**oak**serkurdh/**lahm**erkurdh
pork/veal	**svinekød/kalvekød**	sv**ee**nerkurdh/**kaal**verkurdh
bøf (oksekød)	burf (**oak**serkurdh)	hamburger (beef)
dansk bøf	dahnsk burf	minced beef
engelsk bøf	**ehng**erlsk burf	fillet of beef
frikadeller	freekah**day**lerr	rissoles
hakkebøf	**hahg**gerburf	hamburger
hamburgerryg	hahmb**oo**rerrewg	smoked and glazed pork cutlet
kalve(kotelet)	**kaal**ver(koader**leht**)	veal(cutlet)
kalvebrissel	**kaal**verbreesserl	calf's sweetbreads
koldt kød	kolt kurdh	cold cuts
kødboller	**kurdh**boalerr	meatballs
lam	lahm	lamb
lammebryst	**lahm**erbrewst	breast
lammebov	**lahm**erbo͞o	shoulder
koteletter	koader**leh**derr	chops
lever	**leh**°°err	liver
medisterpølse	mehd**ee**sterrpurlsser	pork sausages
nyrer	n**ew**rerr	kidney
pattegris	**paa**dergreess	sucking-pig
pølser	**purl**serr	sausages
oksesteg	**oak**serstayg	roast beef
ragout	raag**oo**	stew
ribbenssteg	**reebehn**stayg	ribsteak
roastbeef	**roast**beef	roast beef
skinke	**skeen**ker	ham
kogt	koat	boiled
røget	roiert	smoked
svinekød	sv**ee**nerkurdh	pork
flæskesteg	**flehsk**erstayg	roast
mørbrad	**murr**braa	loin
kotelet	koader**leht**	chop
sylte	**sewl**ter	brawn (US headcheese)
tunge	**toong**er	tongue

EATING OUT

How do you like your meat?

baked	**ovnbagt**	o**°°**nbahgt
baked in parchment	**ovnstegt i folie**	o**°°**nstaigt ee **foalyer**
boiled	**kogt**	koat
braised	**grydestegt**	**grewdh**erstaigt
fried	**stegt i panden**	staigt ee **pahnern**
grilled	**grilleret**	grily**āy**rert
roasted	**ovnstegt**	o**°°**nstaigt
sautéed	**brunet i smør**	br**ōō**nert ee smurr
stewed	**stuvet**	st**ōō**ert
underdone	**rødt**	rurt
medium	**medium**	mehd**ēē**oom
well-done	**gennemstegt**	**gehn**ermstaigt

Danish meat dishes

If you have the opportunity to eat in a country inn, you will certainly find some of the most popular national dishes on the menu such as *bøf med løg, frikadeller* and *medisterpølse*, to mention just a few. If you're in the country around Christmas, you might choose, like the Danes, roast pork with cracklings, and for your New Years's menu *hamburgerryg.*

boller i karry
(**boa**ler ee **kaar**ee)
meatballs in a curry sauce accompanied by rice

bøf med løg
(burf maydh lurg)
minced beef and onions served with gravy, boiled potatoes and cucumbers

engelsk bøf
(**ehng**erlsk burf)
fillet of beef with onions and boiled potatoes

flæskesteg med svær
(**flehs**kerstayg maydh svær)
roast pork with cracklings, often served with braised red cabbage, gravy and small browned potatoes

frikadeller
(freekah**day**lerr)
rissoles served with sweet-and-sour cucumber salad or red cabbage and potatoes

hamburgerryg
(hahmb**ōō**rerrewg)
glazed pork cutled (lightly smoked) served with buttered carrots and peas, and boiled potatoes

medisterpølse (mehd**ee**sterrpurlsser)	spiced pork sausage, served with stewed vegetables or sautéed cabbage and potatoes	
sprængt oksebryst (sprehngt **oak**ser- brewst)	boiled, salted brisket of beef, often served with stewed cabbage	
æbleflæsk (**ehb**lerflehsk)	smoked bacon with onions and sautéed apple rings	

Game and fowl

Although some larger restaurants feature game on their
menus throughout the year, the real season for it is autumn,
when it's available in smaller establishments too.

Chicken is common on menus. Game such as pheasants and
grouse are offered for special occasions or holidays. Christmas calls for duck or turkey, unless family tradition demands
roast pork or goose.

I'd like some game.	**Jeg vil gerne have en vildt-anretning.**	yigh veel **gehr**ner hæ ehn **veelt**ahnraytneeng
agerhøne	aaerrh**u**rner	partridge
and (ung)	ahn (oong)	duck(ling)
dyresteg	d**ew**rerstayg	venison
fasan	fahsaan	pheasant
gås	gawss	goose
hare	haarer	hare
hareragout	haarerrahg**oo**	jugged hare
kalkun	kahlk**oo**n	turkey
kanin	kahn**ee**n	rabbit
kylling	**kew**leeng	chicken
bryst	brewst	breast
lår	lor	leg
vinge	**veen**ger	wing
stegt kylling	staigt **kew**leeng	roast chicken
perlehøne	pehrlerh**u**rner	guinea-fowl
rensdyr	rayns**dew**r	reindeer
rype	r**ew**ber	grouse
vagtel	**vahg**terl	quail

EATING OUT

Game and fowl dishes

and, stegt (ahn, staigt)	roast duck stuffed with chestnuts or apples and prunes, served with olive or mushroom sauce
agerhøne (**aa**err**hū**rner)	roast partridge served with chips (US French fries), redcurrant jam or apple sauce, and horseradish
dyreryg med Waldorf-salat (**dēw**rerrewg maydh **vahl**doarfsahlaat)	saddle of venison, served with browned potatoes, poached apple halves filled with jam and accompanied by a salad of celery, walnuts and grapes
fasan, farseret (fah**saan**, fahr**sāy**rert)	stuffed pheasant, served with a cream dressing, mushrooms, potatoes and redcurrant jam
gåsebryst, røget (**gaws**serbrewst, roiert)	smoked breast of goose served with vegetables
kalkunragout (kahlk**ōōn**raag**ōō**)	jugged turkey in a sweet-and-sour gravy, served with mashed potatoes or a chestnut purée
kanin i flødepe- berrod (kahn**ēēn** ee **flū**rdher-peh**°°**rroadh)	jugged rabbit in a horseradish-cream dressing with roast mushroom and onions
kylling, grillstegt (**kew**leeng, grilstaigt)	grilled chicken with green salad or sweet-and-sour cucumber salad and chips (US French fries)

Most game dishes are garnished with a tasty brown sauce and accompanied by potatoes and redcurrant or cranberry jam.

Vegetables and noodles

What vegetables do you recommend?	**Hvilke grønsager anbefaler De?**	vilker **grurn**saaerr **ahn**berfaalerr dee
I'd prefer some salad.	**Jeg vil hellere have en salat.**	yigh veel **hay**lerrer hæ ehn sah**laat**
artiskokker	ahr**tees**koaggerr	artichokes
asparges(hoveder)	ah**spahrs**(ho**°°**erdherr)	asparagus (tips)
blomkål	**bloam**kawl	cauliflower
champignons	**shahm**peenyoan	mushrooms

grønne bønner	grurner burnerr	haricot (French) beans
græskar	graiskahr	marrow
gulerødder	gōōlerrurdherr	carrots
hvide bønner	veedher burnerr	kidney beans
hvidløg	veedhlurg	garlic
julesalat	yōōlersahlaat	chicory
kartofler	kahrtoaflerr	potatoes
linser	leensserr	lentils
løg	lurg	onions
majs	mighss	sweet corn
majskolbe	mighskoalber	corn on the cob
nudler	noodlerr	noodles
peberfrugt	peh°°errfroogt	peppers
persille	payrseeler	parsley
porrer	poarerr	leeks
ris	rēēss	rice
rosenkål	rōässernkawl	Brussels sprouts
rødbeder	rurdhbehdherr	beetroot
rødkål	rurdhkawl	red cabbage
salat	sahlaat	lettuce, salad
salatagurk	sahlaatahgoork	cucumbers
selleri	sehlerree	celery
spinat	speenaat	spinach
tomater	toamaaderr	tomatoes
trøfler	trurflerr	truffles
turnips	toorneeps	turnips
ærter	ærterr	peas

Here are some of the ways in which your vegetables may be served:

baked	ovnbagt	o°°nbahgt
diced	skåret i terninger	skoarert ee tāyrneenger
fried	stegt	staigt
grilled	grilleret	grilyāyrert
stewed	stuvet	stōōert
stuffed	fyldt	fewlt

EATING OUT

Sauces and preparations

With meat:

ansjossmør (ahnshōāssmurr)	anchovy butter
bearnaisesovs (berahrnaissoʳʳss)	a cream dressing flavoured with tarragon and vinegar
chutney-smør ("chutney"-smurr)	chutney butter
flødepeberrod (flūrdherpehʳʳerroadh)	horseradish cream dressing
hvidløgssmør (veedhlurgssmurr)	garlic butter
remoulade (rehmoalaadher)	mustard and herb cream dressing

Warm preparations:

løgsovs (lurgsoʳʳss)	onion sauce
kastaniesovs (kahstahnyersoʳʳss)	chestnut sauce, flavoured with madeira wine
sellerisovs (sehlerreesoʳʳss)	celery flavoured sauce with sherry
sennepssovs (sehnerpsoʳʳss)	mustard sauce
vildtsovs (veeltsoʳʳss)	a sauce made with fresh cream and redcurrant jam

And as a garnish to many a meat dish, you will certainly encounter:

asier (aasherr)	cucumbers, marinated in vinegar and sugar

With salads:

If you order a salad, you'll probably have the choice of the following dressings:

citronmarinade (seetrōānmaareenaidher)	lemon, oil, salt and pepper, paprika, herbs
vinaigrette-sovs (veenaigreht-soʳʳss)	vinegar, oil, salt and pepper, possibly French mustard, and onions or garlic

stærk salatsovs (stærk sahlaat-soº°ss)	egg yolks, vinegar or lemon juice, oil, salt and pepper or paprika, Worcester sauce, onion or garlic and dill, all mixed with whipped cream
ymersovs (ewmerrsoº°ss)	lemon juice, spices and herbs, mixed with milk or cream

With desserts:

appelsinsovs (ahberlseensoº°ss)	orange sauce
hvidvinssovs (veedhveensoº°ss)	white-wine sauce
råcreme (rawkraym)	"raw cream"—egg, sugar, whipped cream and vanilla, sometimes flavoured with sherry, liqueur or cognac

Cheese

danablu (daanaabloo)	Danish blue cheese, rich with a sharp flavour
danbo (dahnboa)	a mild, firm cheese with holes, sometimes flavoured with caraway seeds
elbo (ehlboa)	a hard cheese with a delicate taste
esrom (aysroam)	a mild, slightly aromatic cheese of spongy texture
fynbo (fewnboa)	a very mild, rich cheese similar to samsø (see below)
havarti (haavahrtee)	semi-hard, with a piquant flavour
maribo (mahreeboa)	a soft, mild cheese
molbo (moalboa)	not unlike edam; rich and highly flavoured
mycella (mewssehlah)	similar to Danish blue cheese, but milder; the veins are greenish-blue
samsø (sahmsur)	a mild, firm cheese with a sweet, nutty flavour

There are also excellent imitations of *camembert, brie, emmentaler* and other French or Swiss cheeses.

EATING OUT

Fruit

Fruit is generally served after the cheese.

Do you have fresh fruit.	**Har De frisk frugt?**	haar dee freesk froogt
I'd like a (fresh) fruit salad.	**Jeg vil gerne have en (frisk) frugt-salat.**	yigh veel **gehr**ner hæ ehn (freesk) **froogt**-sahlaat

abrikoser	ahbree**koass**err	apricots
ananas	**ah**nahnahss	pineapple
appelsiner	ahberl**seen**err	oranges
bananer	baa**naan**err	bananas
blommer	**bloam**err	plums
blåbær	**blaw**bær	blueberries
brombær	**broam**bær	blackberries
citron	seet**roan**	lemon
dadler	**dahd**hlerr	dates
ferskner	**fayr**sknerr	peaches
figner	**fee**nerr	figs
grapefrugt	"grape"-froogt	grapefruit
græskar	**grai**skahr	pumpkin
hasselnødder	**hah**sserlnurdherr	hazelnuts
hindbær	**heen**bær	raspberries
jordbær	**yoar**bær	strawberries
kastanier	kah**stah**nyerr	chestnuts
kirsebær	**keers**serbær	cherries
kvæder	**kvai**dherr	quinces
mandariner	mahndaah**reen**err	tangerines
mandler	**mahn**lerr	almonds
melon	meh**loan**	melon
nødder	**nur**dherr	nuts
(blandede)	(**blaan**dherdher)	(assorted)
pærer	**pær**err	pears
rabarber	rah**bahr**berr	rhubarb
ribs	reebss	redcurrants
rosiner	roas**seen**err	raisins
solbær	**soal**bær	blackcurrants
stikkelsbær	**stig**gerlsbær	gooseberries
svesker	**sveh**skerr	prunes
tyttebær	**tew**derbær	cranberries
valnødder	**vahl**nurdherr	walnuts
vandmelon	**vahn**mehloan	watermelon
vindruer	**veen**drōoerr	grapes
æbler	**ehb**lerr	apples

Dessert

If you've survived all the courses on the menu, you may want to say:

| I'd like a dessert, please. | **Jeg vil gerne have en dessert.** | yigh veel **gehr**ner hæ ehn deh**ss**ayrt |
| Something light, please. | **Jeg vil gerne have noget let.** | yigh veel **gehr**ner hæ nōāert leht |

If you aren't sure...

| What do you have for dessert? | **Hvad kan man få til dessert?** | vahdh kehn mahn faw til deh**ss**ayrt |

Here are a few desserts to tempt your sweet tooth:

| **æblekage med rasp og flødeskum** (ehblerkaaer maydh rahsp oa flūrdher-skoom) | stewed apples with vanilla served with alternating layers of biscuit-crumbs and topped with whipped cream |
| **bondepige med slør** (boanerpēēer maydh slurr) | "veiled country maid"; a mixture of rye-bread crumbs, apple sauce, cream and sugar |

fromage	froamaasher	mousse
appelsinfromage	ahberlsēēnfroamaasher	orange-mousse
citronfromage	seetrōānfroamaasher	lemon-mousse
is	ēēss	ice-cream
chokoladeis	shoakoalaadherēēss	chocolate ice-cream
jordbæris	yoarbærēēss	strawberry ice-cream
vanilleis	vaaneelyerēēss	vanilla ice-cream
med flødeskum	maydh flūrdherskoom	with whipped cream
kage	kaaer	cake
flødekage	flūrdherkaaer	layer cream cake
lagkage	lahgkaaer	layer cake
småkager	smawkaaerr	biscuits (US cookies)
tørkage	turrkaaer	plain cake
karamelrand	kahrahmaylrahn	caramel custard
pandekager	pahnerkaaer	pancakes
små pandekager	smaw pahnerkaaerr	fritters
ris à l'amande	rēēss ahlahmahng	rice and almond pudding with fruit sauce
rødgrød med fløde	rurdhgrurdh maydh flūrdher	fruit jelly served with cream

The bill

I'd like to pay.	**Jeg vil gerne betale.**	yigh veel **gehr**ner bertaaler
We'd like to pay separately.	**Vi vil gerne betale hver for sig.**	vee veel **gehr**ner bertaaler vayr foar sigh
You've made a mistake in this bill, I think.	**De har vist lavet en fejl på regningen.**	dee haar veest **laav**ert ehn fighl paw **righ**neenern
What is this amount for?	**Hvad dækker dette beløb?**	vahdh **dehg**gerr **deh**der behlurp

Note: Service and other charges are always included.

Do you accept traveller's cheques?	**Tager De imod rejsechecks?**	taar dee ee**moadh** **righ**sserchayks
Thank you, this is for you.	**Værsågod.**	værsawgoadh
Keep the change.	**Behold resten.**	ber**hoal** **ray**stern
That was a very good meal.	**Det var et dejligt måltid.**	day vaar eht **digh**leet **mawl**teedh
We enjoyed it, thank you.	**Vi har nydt det.**	vee haar newt day

---

BETJENING IBEREGNET
SERVICE INCLUDED

Complaints

But perhaps you'll have something to complain about:

That's not what I ordered. I asked for...	**Det har jeg ikke bestilt. Jeg bad om...**	day haar yigh **igg**er ber**steelt**. yigh bahdh oam
May I change this?	**Må jeg bytte dette?**	maw yigh **bewd**er **deh**der
The meat is...	**Kødet er...**	**kurdh**ert ayr
overdone	**stegt for meget**	staigt foar **migh**ert
underdone	**stegt for lidt**	staigt foar lidt
too rare	**for råt**	foar rot
too tough	**for sejt**	foar sight

This is too...	**Dette er for...**	dehder ayr foar
bitter/salty/sweet	**bittert/salt/sødt**	biderrt/sahlt/surtt
The food is cold.	**Maden er kold.**	maadhern ayr kol
This isn't fresh.	**Dette er ikke friskt.**	dehder ayr igger freeskt
What's taking you so long?	**Hvorfor varer det så længe?**	vorfor vāērerr day saw lainger
Where are our drinks?	**Hvor bliver vore drinks af?**	vōar blēēerr vōārer drinks ah
This isn't clean.	**Dette er ikke rent.**	dehder ayr igger raynt
Would you ask the head waiter to come over?	**Vil De kalde på overtjeneren?**	veel dee kahler paw o°° ertyāynerrern

Drinks

In common with the other Scandinavian countries, Denmark has strict regulations governing the purchase and consumption of alcoholic beverages. Liquor is heavily taxed, so if you travel by boat you will notice that the duty-free bars on board do a lively trade. Here or at an airport duty-free shop is where you should buy your quota. Even if you are a non-drinker, the bottle will make a highly appreciated gift.

Beer

The Carlsberg and Tuborg breweries are known all over the world. But there are many others producing good, strong beer, so when travelling in Denmark, try some of the local brews.

Incidentally, many breweries will be only too pleased to show you around—and to let you sample their products!

Many different types of beer are found in restaurants and liquor stores. *Pilsner* (**pils**nerr) is a light beer, while *lager* (**laa**err) is the term used in Denmark to denote a somewhat darker beer. The word "export" on the label usually indicates a beer of higher alcoholic content.

EATING OUT

Akvavit—Snaps

Call it *akvavit* (ahkvah**veet)** or simply *snaps* (snahpss).
Along with beer, it's the national drink of Denmark. Like
vodka, it's distilled from potatoes, though barley is also
used. The colour varies according to the herbs and spices
with which the drink is flavoured.

Akvavit should be drunk ice-cold from thimble-sized glasses.
It is often washed down with a beer chaser. It accompanies a
meal and is never used in mixed drinks.

Other alcoholic drinks

You'll be able to get any kind of drink you desire. And
you'll have no difficulty in ordering, because the Danish and
English names for most of them are the same. American-
style cocktails are foreign to the Danish way of life, but you
can obtain them in any good bar.

glass	**et glas**	eht glahss
bottle	**en flaske**	ehn **flah**sker
neat (straight)	**tør**	turr
on the rocks	**med isterninger**	maydh $\overline{ee}$sst**ay**rneengerr

After your meal, don't miss the famous cherry liqueur,
Cherry Heering (named after the Heering family, not the
herring). Or you may feel like:

brandy	**en brandy**	ehn **brahn**dee
fruit-distilled	**frugt-destilleret**	froogt-dehsteel**ay**rert
apple	**calvados**	kahlvah**doass**
cherry brandy	**cherry brandy**	"cherry brandy"
cognac	**en cognac**	ehn "cognac"
cordial liqueur	**en likør**	ehn leek**ur**
port	**en portvin**	ehn **poart**v$\overline{ee}$n

SKÅL!

(skawl)

CHEERS!

Wine

Denmark is not a wine-producing country. Wine, mostly imported from France, Italy, Portugal and Spain, has gained in popularity recently due to decreasing prices, and is widely available.

Ask the waiter for the wine list: *Må jeg få vinkortet* (maw yigh faw **vēēn**koartert).

I'd like a...of...	**Jeg vil gerne have...**	yigh veel **geh**rner hæ
glass	**et glas**	eht glahss
carafe	**en karaffel**	ehn kah**rah**ferl
half bottle	**en halv flaske**	ehn hahl **flahs**ker
bottle	**en flaske**	ehn **flahs**ker
litre	**en liter**	ehn **lee**derr
I want a bottle of white/red wine.	**Jeg ønsker en flaske hvid-/rødvin.**	yigh **urns**kerr ehn **flahs**ker veedh-/**rurdh**vēēn
Do you have open wine?	**Har De åben vin?**	haar dee **aw**bern vēēn

If you enjoyed the wine, you may want to say:

Please bring me another...	**Vær venlig at bringe en...til.**	vær **veh**nlee aht **bring**er ehn...til

red	**rød**	rurdh
white	**hvid**	veedh
rosé	**rosé**	roas**sāy**
very dry	**meget tør**	**migh**ert turr
dry	**tør**	turr
sweet	**sød**	surdh
light	**let**	leht
full-bodied	**fyldig**	**fewl**dee
sparkling	**mousserende**	moos**sāy**rerner
chilled	**afkølet**	**ow**kurlert
at room temperature	**tempereret**	taympehr**āy**rert

Other beverages

(hot) chocolate	(varm) chokolade	(vahrm) shoakoalaadher
coffee	kaffe	kahfer
coffee with cream	kaffe med fløde	kahfer maydh flurdher
expresso	espresso	"espresso"
fruit juice	frugtsaft	froogtsahft
apple/grapefruit	æble/grapefrugt	ehbler/"grape"-froogt
lemon/orange	citron/appelsin	seetroan/ahberlseen
pineapple/tomato	ananas/tomat	ahnahnahss/toamaat
lemonade	limonade	leemoanaadher
milk	mælk	mehlk
mineral water	mineralvand	meenerraalvahn
orangeade	appelsinvand	ahberlseenvahn
soda water	sodavand	soadahvahn
squash (soda pop)	squash	"squash"
tea	te	teh
with milk	med mælk	maydh mehlk
with lemon	med citron	maydh seetroan
iced tea	iste	eessteh
tonic water	tonicvand	tonikvahn

Eating light—Snacks

Please give me a/an some...	Må jeg bede om...	maw yigh bay oam
biscuits (Br.)	nogle småkager	noaler smawkaaerr
bread	noget brød	noaert brurdh
butter	noget smør	noaert smurr
cake	en kage	ehn kaaer
candy	nogle søde sager/bolsjer	noaler surdher saaerr/boalsherr
chocolate bar	en plade chokolade	ehn plaadher shoakoalaadher
cookies	nogle småkager	noaler smawkaaerr
Danish pastry	et stykke wiener-brød	eht stewgger veenerr-brurdh
frankfurter	nogle pølser	noaler purlsserr
hamburger	en bøfsandwich	ehn burf "sandwich"
ice-cream	en is	ehn eess
pastry	en kage	ehn kaaer
rolls	nogle rundstykker	noaler roonstewgger
sweets	nogle søde sager/bolsjer	noaler surdher saaerr/boalsherr
How much is that?	Hvor meget bliver det?	voar mighert bleeerr day

Travelling around

Plane

In addition to Copenhagen's international airport of Kastrup there are eleven domestic airports in Denmark. Several flights daily link Kastrup with each of the other centres. For most destinations abroad the fares from Jutland, Funen and Bornholm are the same as from Kastrup.

Is there a flight to Paris?	**Er der et fly til Paris?**	ayr dayr eht flew til pahreess
Is it a nonstop flight?	**Er det direkte?**	ayr day deeraykter
When's the next plane to Rønne?	**Hvornår afgår næste fly til Rønne?**	vornawr owgawr nehster flew til Rurner
Do I have to change planes?	**Skal jeg skifte maskine?**	skahl yigh skeefter mahskeener
Can I get to Billund today?	**Kan jeg flyve til Billund i dag?**	kehn yigh flewer til beeloon ee dai
I'd like a ticket to Copenhagen.	**Jeg vil gerne have en billet til København.**	yigh veel gehrner hæ ehn beelayt til kurbernhown
What's the fare to Aalborg?	**Hvad koster det til Ålborg?**	vahdh koasterr day til awlboar
single (one-way) return (roundtrip) economy/first class	**en enkeltbillet en returbillet turist/første klasse**	ehn aynkerltbeelayt ehn raytoorbeelayt tooreest/furrster klaasser
Is there an excursion fare?	**Findes der rabat-billetter?**	finnerss dayr rahbaht-beelayderr
What time do I have to check in?	**Hvornår skal man være der?**	vornawr skahl mahn værer dayr
What time do we arrive?	**Hvornår ankommer vi?**	vornawr ahnkoamerr vee

ANKOMST	AFGANG
ARRIVAL	DEPARTURE

TRAVELLING AROUND

Surface transport

Buses and coaches provide an extension to the rail network in serving the smaller towns. They also offer excursions to the countryside. Intercity bus connections are recommendable for shorter distances; not only are they cheaper than the train, but they offer prettier scenery. However, for long distances the train is faster and more comfortable. If in doubt, ask the advice of the local tourist office, a travel agency or your hotel desk-clerk.

Train

The geographical composition of the country makes ferry boats necessary for rail connections between Jutland and the islands. This introduces a pleasant element of variety into long trips. Considerable reductions are granted to students, children (free up to four years of age), groups, families and "senior citizens" (over the age of 65). Trains and ferries have first and second-class coaches, and long-distance night trains have sleeping-cars.

Types of trains

Intercity ("intercity")	long-distance express. Seat reservation required when crossing the Great Belt
Lyntog (**lewn**toa)	long-distance express. Seat reservation required; supplementary fare
Eksprestog (ayks**prayss**toa)	long-distance train, stopping at main stations
Persontog (payrs**ōān**toa)	local train, stopping at all stations
Sovevogn (**so**°°ervoan)	sleeping car operated on international trains; individual compartments (single or double) and washing facilities
Liggevogn (**leegg**ervoan)	berth with blankets and pillows *(couchette)* on long-distance night trains

TRAVELLING AROUND

Godsvogn	guard's van (baggage car)
(**goass**voan)	
Togfærge	train ferries (the train drives onto the boat)
(**toa**fairgger)	to Funen, Jutland, Sweden, and across the
	Baltic to the South

To the railway station

Where's the railway station?	**Hvor ligger bane-gården?**	v**ōā**r **liggerr bæner-gawr**ern
Taxi, please!	**Taxi!**	**tah**ksi
Take me to the rail-way station.	**Kør mig til bane-gården.**	k**ū̄**r may til **bæner-gawr**ern
What's the fare?	**Hvor meget bliver det?**	v**ōā**r **mighert bl**ē**ē**err day

INDGANG	ENTRANCE
UDGANG	EXIT
TIL PERRONERNE	TO THE PLATFORMS

Where's the...?

Where is/are the...?	**Hvor er...?**	v**ōā**r ayr
bar	**baren**	**bahr**ern
barber's shop	**frisøren**	frees**ū̄r**rern
booking office	**pladsbestillingen**	**plahss**bersteeleengern
currency exchange office	**vekselkontoret**	**vayks**erlkoant**ōā**rert
left luggage office (baggage check)	**garderoben**	gahrderr**ōā**bern
lost-property (lost and found) office	**hittegodskontoret**	**heed**ergoasskoant**ōā**rert
luggage lockers	**autoboksene**	**owtoa**boakserner
news-stand	**aviskiosken**	ahv**ēē**skyoaskern
platform 7	**perron 7**	**pay**rong 7
reservations office	**pladsbestillingen**	**plahss**bersteeleengern
snack bar	**snackbaren**	**snæk**bahrern
ticket office	**billetkontoret**	beelaytkoant**ōā**rert
waiting-room	**ventesalen**	**vaynt**ersaalern
Where are the toilets?	**Hvor er toilettet?**	v**ōā**r ayr toaee**lay**dert

FOR TAXI, see page 27

TRAVELLING AROUND

Inquiries

In Denmark ⓘ means information office.

When is the...train to Aarhus?	**Hvornår afgår det... tog til Århus?**	vornawr owgawr day... toa til awrhōōss
first/last/next	**første/sidste/ næste**	furrster/seester/ nehster
What time does the train for Randers leave?	**Hvornår afgår toget til Randers?**	vornawr owgawr toaert til rahnerss
What's the fare to Middelfart?	**Hvad koster det til Middelfart?**	vahdh koasterr day til meedherlfahrt
Is it a through train?	**Er det gennem- gående tog?**	ayr day eht gehnerm- gawerner toa
Will the train leave on time?	**Afgår toget efter planen?**	owgawr toaert ehfterr plaanern
Is the train late?	**Er toget forsinket?**	ayr toaert forseenkert
What time does the train arrive at Roskilde?	**Hvornår ankommer toget til Roskilde?**	vornawr ahnkoamer toaert til roaskeeller
Is there a dining car on the train?	**Er der spisevogn i toget?**	ayr dayr spēēsservoan ee toaert
Is there a sleeping car on the train?	**Er der sovevogn i toget?**	ayr dayr so°°ervoan ee toaert
Does the train stop at Horsens?	**Standser toget i Horsens?**	stahnserr toaert ee hoarsernss
What platform does the train for Helsingør leave from?	**Fra hvilket spor afgår toget til Helsingør?**	fraa vilkert spoar owgawr toaert til haylseengurr
What platform does the train from... arrive at?	**På hvilket spor ankommer toget fra...?**	paw vilkert spoar ahnkoamer toaert fraa

---

TURISTBUREAU	TOURIST INFORMATION
VEKSLING	CURRENCY EXCHANGE
FREMMED VALUTA	CURRENCY EXCHANGE

Det er et gennemgående tog.	It's a through train.
De skal skifte i...	You have to change at...
Spor...er...	Platform...is...
derovre/ovenpå	over there/upstairs
til venstre/til højre	on the left/on the right
Der afgår et tog til... klokken...	There's a train to... at...
Deres tog afgår fra spor...	Your train will leave from platform...
Toget er forsinket... minutter.	There'll be a delay of... minutes.

Tickets

I want a ticket to Copenhagen.	Jeg vil gerne have en billet til København.	yigh veel **gehr**ner hæ ehn **bee**layt til kurbern**hown**
single (one-way)	enkelt	**ayn**kerlt
return (roundtrip)	retur	ray**toor**
first/second class	første/anden klasse	**furr**ster/**ah**nern **klaass**er
Must the boy/girl pay the full fare?	Skal drengen/pigen betale fuld pris?	skahl **drayng**ern/**pee**ern ber**taal**er fool **preess**
I'd like to reserve a seat.	Jeg vil gerne reservere en plads.	yigh veel **gehr**ner rayssehr**vay**rer ehn **plahss**
I'm a student/ I'm over 65. Do I get a reduction?	Jeg er studerende/ Jeg er over 65. Kan jeg få billet til nedsat pris?	yigh ayr stoo**day**rerner/ yigh ayr o°°er 65. kehn yigh faw **bee**layt til **nāydh**saht **preess**

Første eller anden klasse?	First or second class?
Enkelt eller retur-billet?	Single or return (one-way or roundtrip)?
Hvor gammel er han/hun?	How old is he/she?

All aboard

Is this the right platform for the train to Copenhagen?	**Afgår toget til København fra dette spor?**	owgawr toaert til kurbernhown fraa dehder spoar
Is this the right train to Odense?	**Er det her toget til Odense?**	ayr day hayr toaert til oadhernsser
Excuse me. May I get by?	**Undskyld, må jeg komme forbi?**	oonskewl maw yigh koamer foarbee
Is this seat taken?	**Er denne plads optaget?**	ayr dehner plahss optaaert

---

IKKE-RYGERE
NO SMOKING

I think that's my seat.	**Det er vist min plads.**	day ayr veesst meen plahss
Would you let me know before we get to Fredericia?	**Vil De sige til, før vi ankommer til Fredericia?**	veel dee seeer til furr vee ahnkoamerr til fraydherray_sseeah
What station is this?	**Hvad hedder denne station?**	vahdh hehdherr dehner stahsyoan
How long does the train stop here?	**Hvor længe holder toget her?**	voar lainger hoalerr toaert hayr
When do we get to Kolding?	**Hvornår ankommer vi til Kolding?**	vornawr ahnkoamerr vee til koleeng

Sometime on the journey the ticket collector (*togkontrolløren*—**toa**kontroalurrern) will come around and say: *Må jeg se Deres billetter?* (Tickets, please!).

Eating

There are no dining cars on Danish trains, though snacks can be obtained on intercity and express trains.

Most rail travel in Denmark requires taking a ferry, on which dining and/or cafeteria facilities are always provided.

Ferries crossing *Storebælt* have restaurants; they serve hot and cold meals. You should find a table before sailing time if you want to finish your meal; the voyage only lasts about an hour.

| Where can I get something to eat/drink? | **Hvor kan jeg få noget at spise/drikke?** | vōār kehn yigh faw nōāert aht spēēsser/drigger |

Sleeping

Are there any free compartments in the sleeping car?	**Er der ledige kupeer i sovevognen?**	ayr dayr lehdhēēer koo-pāyerr ee so°°ervoanern
Where's the sleeping car?	**Hvor er sove-vognen?**	vōār ayr so°°ervoanern
Where's my berth?	**Hvor er min køje?**	vōār ayr mēēn koier
Compartments 18 and 19, please.	**Hvor finder jeg kupé nr. 18 og 19?**	vōār finnerr yigh koopāy noommerr 18 oa 19
I'd like an upper/lower berth.	**Jeg vil gerne have den øverste/nederste køje.**	yigh veel gehrner hæ dehn ūrverrster/nāydherster koier
Would you make up our berths?	**Vil De være venlig at rede op?**	veel dee vāerer vehnlee aht raydher op
Would you call me at 7 o'clock?	**Vil De vække mig klokken 7?**	veel dee vehgger migh kloaggern 7
Would you bring me some coffee in the morning?	**Vil De bringe mig kaffe i morgen tidlig?**	veel dee bringer migh kahfer ee mōāern teedhlee

Baggage and porters

| Can you help me with my bags? | **Kan De tage Dem af min bagage?** | kehn dee tæ dehm ah mēēn bahgaasher |
| Please put them down here. | **Vær venlig at stille dem her.** | vāēr vehnlee aht steeler dehm hayr |

Note: For an extra charge you may have your baggage sent as *rejsegods* (**righs**sergoass) in the guard's van (baggage car) to be claimed at the end of the trip.

FOR PORTERS, see also page 24

Lost!

We hope you'll have no need for the following phrases on your trip...but just in case:

Where's the lost property office (lost and found)?	**Hvor er hittegods-kontoret?**	vōar ayr **heed**ergoass-koant**ōā**rert
I've lost my...	**Jeg har mistet min...**	yigh haar **mee**stert mēēn
this morning	**i morges**	ee **mōā**rerss
yesterday	**i går**	ee gawr
I lost it in...	**Jeg mistede den i...**	yigh **mee**sterdher dehn ee

Timetables

If you intend to do a lot of rail travel, buy one of the compact, country-wide timetables on sale at ticket and inquiry offices and in some bookshops.

I'd like to buy a timetable.	**Jeg vil gerne købe en køreplan.**	yigh veel **gehr**ner k**ūr**ber ehn k**ūr**rerplaan

Underground (subway)

Copenhagen's *S-bane* is the equivalent of the London underground or the New York subway. A route map is displayed outside every station. The *S-bane* operates from 5 a.m. till 12.30 at night. Tickets are interchangeable on buses and trains. Children under 4 travel free and from 4–12 at half fare. Tickets must be stamped in the automatic machines on the platform before you board the train. You will recognize *S-bane* stations by a winged *S* sign at the entrance.

Where's the nearest underground station?	**Hvor er den nærmeste S-tog station?**	vōar ayr dehn **nær**merster s-toa stahs**yoan**
Does this train go to...?	**Går dette tog til...?**	gawr **dehd**er toa til
Where do I change for...?	**Hvor skal jeg skifte til...?**	vōar skahl yigh **skeef**ter til
Is the next station...?	**Er næste station...?**	ayr **neh**ster stahs**yoan**

Bus

All major cities have excellent bus service. For a single trip
you can buy your ticket on the bus. If you plan to make
intensive use of the bus you'll find it cheaper to buy a multi-
journey card *(rabatkort*—rah**baht**koart). They can be pur-
chased at railway stations and some hotels.

There is also an extensive coach network reaching all parts
of the country.

A ticket to ..., please.	**En billet til ...**	ehn beel**ayd** til
Where can I get a bus to Tivoli?	**Hvor holder bussen til Tivoli?**	vōār **hoal**err **booss**ern til **teev**oalee
What bus do I take for the...Hotel?	**Hvilken bus går til Hotel...?**	**vilk**ern booss gawr til ho**a**tayl
Where's the bus stop/terminus?	**Hvor er busstoppe-stedet/ende-stationen?**	vōār ayr **booss**stobberst**ā**y-dhert/**ehn**derstahssyoanern
When is the...bus to Valby?	**Hvornår går den... bus til Valby?**	vornawr gawr dehn... booss til **vaal**bew
first/last/next	**første/sidste/næste**	**furr**ster/**seest**er/**neh**ster
How often do the buses go to the royal palace?	**Hvor ofte går der bus til Amalienborg Slot?**	vōār **oaft**er gawr dayr booss til ahmail**ēē**ernboar sloat
How much is the fare to...?	**Hvad koster billetten til...?**	vahdh **koast**err bee-**layd**ern til
Do I have to change buses?	**Skal jeg skifte bus?**	skahl yigh **skeef**ter booss
How long does the journey take?	**Hvor længe varer rejsen?**	vōār **lain**ger v**æ**rerr **righ**ssern
Will you tell me when to get off?	**Vil De sige til, når jeg skal af?**	veel dee **sēē**er til nawr yigh skahl ah
I want to get off at the Cathedral.	**Jeg vil gerne af ved domkirken.**	yigh veel **gehr**ner ah vaydh **doam**keerkern

BUSSTOP	REGULAR BUS STOP
STOP PÅ FORLANGENDE	STOPS ON REQUEST

Is there a coach to …?	**Er der en rutebil til …?**	ayr dayr ehn r**ōō**derb**ēē**l til
Please let me off at the next stop.	**Jeg vil gerne af ved næste stoppested.**	yigh veel **gehr**ner ah vaydh **neh**ster stobber-st**ā**ydh
May I please have my luggage?	**Kan jeg få min bagage?**	kehn yigh faw m**ēē**n bah**gaa**sher

Boat services

Jutland, the Danish islands, Norway, Sweden, England, East and West Germany can be reached by ship or car ferry. Since the major Danish cities are located on the coast, intercity trips can also be made by ferry. On the main shipping routes it's advisable to reserve both car space and cabins well in advance. This can be done through any travel agency.

Other modes of transport

bicycle	**en cykel**	ehn **sewg**gerl
boat	**en båd**	ehn bawdh
houseboat	**husbåd**	h**ōō**ssbawdh
motorboat	**motorbåd**	m**ōā**toarbawdh
rowing boat	**robåd**	roabawdh
sailing boat	**sejlbåd**	**sighl**bawdh
car ferry	**en bilfærge**	ehn b**ēē**lfæryer
ferry	**en færge**	ehn færyer
helicopter	**en helikopter**	ehn hayleekopterr
hitchhiking	**tage på tommelfinger**	taaer paw **toam**erlfeengerr
horseriding	**til hest**	til hayst
hovercraft	**en flyvebåd**	ehn flewvverbawdh
moped (motor-bike)	**en knallert**	ehn **knah**lert
motorcycle	**en motorcykel**	ehn m**ōā**toarsewggerl

And if you're really stuck, start …

| walking | **til fods** | til foass |

(For more information on cycling, walking, riding and sailing possibilities, see pages 85–86.)

Around and about—Sightseeing

Here we're more concerned with the cultural aspect of life
than with entertainment; and, for the moment, with towns
rather than the countryside. If you want a guide book,
ask...

Can you recommend a guide book on...?	**Kan De anbefale en god turisthåndbog over...?**	kehn dee **ahn**berfaaler ehn goadh too**reest**hawn-bōā o°°er
Where's the tourist office?	**Hvor er turistbureauet?**	vōār ayr too**reest**bewroaert
What are the main points of interest?	**Hvilke steder har særlig interesse?**	vilkert **stay**dherr haar **sær**lee interr**ays**ser
We're here for...	**Vi bliver her...**	vee bl**ēē**err hayr
only a few hours	**kun et par timer**	koon eht pahr t**ēē**merr
a day	**en dag**	ehn dai
3 days	**3 dage**	3 **dai**er
a week	**en uge**	ehn **ōō**er
Can you recommend a (city) sightseeing tour?	**Kan De anbefale en (by)rundtur?**	kehn de **ahn**berfaaler ehn (bew)**roon**tōōr
Where does the bus start from?	**Hvor starter bussen?**	vōār **stahr**terr **booss**ern
Will it pick us up at the hotel?	**Henter den os ved hotellet?**	**hayn**terr dehn oss vaydh **hoa**taylert
What bus should we take?	**Hvilken bus skal vi tage?**	vilkern booss skahl vee tæ
How much does the tour cost?	**Hvad koster turen?**	vahdh **koas**terr t**ōō**rern
What time does the tour start?	**Hvornår begynder turen?**	vornawr ber**gew**ner t**ōō**rern
What time do we get back?	**Hvornår kommer vi tilbage?**	vornawr **koa**merr vee til**baa**er
We'd like to rent a car for the day.	**Vi vil gerne leje en bil for i dag.**	vee veel **gehr**ner **ligh**er ehn b**ēē**l foar ee dai
Is there an English-speaking guide?	**Taler rejseføreren engelsk?**	**tai**lerr **righs**serf**ūū**rerr-ern **ehng**erlsk

FOR TIME OF DAY, see page 178

Where is/Where are the...?	Hvor er...?	vōar ayr
amusement park	forlystelsesparken (Tivoli or Bakken)	forlewsterlsserspahrkern (tivoalee*or*bahkern)
aquarium	akvariet	ahkvaarēēert
art gallery	kunstgalleriet	koonstgahlerrēēert
artist's quarter	kunstnernes kvarter	koonstnerrnerss kvahrtāyr
beach	stranden	strahnern
botanical gardens	Botanisk Have	boataaneesk haaver
brewery	bryggeriet	brewggerrēēert
bridge	broen	broaern
building	bygningen	bewgneengern
business district	forretningskvarteret	foarraytneengskvahrtāyrert
castle	slottet	sloadert
cathedral	domkirken	doamkeerkern
cemetery	kirkegården	keerkergawrern
city centre	bycentret	bēwsayntrert
city hall	rådhuset	rawdhhōōssert
church	kirken	keerkern
concert hall	koncertsalen	koansayrtsaalern
creek	åen	awern
docks	kajerne	kigherner
downtown area	bycentret	bēwsayntrert
exhibition	udstillingen	ōōdhsteeleengern
fortress	fæstningen	fehstneengern
fountain	springvandet	springvahnert
gardens	haven	haavern
harbour	havnen	hownern
lake	søen	sūrern
library	biblioteket	bibleeoatehggert
market	torvet	toarvert
memorial	mindesmærket	meenersmærkert
mermaid statue	Den lille Havfrue	dehn leeler howfrōōer
monument	monumentet	moanoomehntert
museum	museet	moossehert
observatory	observatoriet	obsehrvaatōōrēēert
old town	den gamle by	dehn gahmler bēw
opera house	operaen	oapehraaern
palace	slottet	sloadert
park	parken	pahrkern
parliament building	regeringsbygningen (Christiansborg Slot)	rehgehreengsbewgneengern (kreesteeeahnsboar sloat)
planetarium	planetariet	plaanertaarēēert

FOR ASKING THE WAY, see page 144

royal palace	kongeslottet	koangersloadert
	(Amalienborg Slot)	(ahmailēēernboar sloat)
royal theatre	Det kongelige Teater	day koangerlēēer tehahterr
seafront	søbredden	sūrbraydhern
shopping centre	indkøbscentret	inkūrbssayntrert
stadium	stadion	stadyon
statue	statuen	statōōern
swimming pool	svømmebadet	svurmerbaadhert
synagogue	synagogen	sewnaagōāern
theatre	teatret	tehahtrert
tomb	gravstedet	growstaydhert
tower	tårnet	tawrnert
university	universitetet	ooneevehrseetāȳdert
watermill	vandmøllen	vahnmurlern
windmill	vindmøllen	vinmurlern
zoo	Zoologisk Have	soaloaggeesk haaver

Admission

Is...open on Sundays?	Er...åben om søndagen?	ayr...awbern oam surndaiern
When does it open/close?	Hvornår åbnes/lukkes der?	vornawr awbnoroo/looggerss dayr
Where do I get tickets?	Hvor kan jeg købe billetter?	vōar kehn yigh kūrber beelayderr
How much is the entrance fee?	Hvor meget koster det i entré?	vōar mighert koasterr day ee ahntray
Is there any reduction for students/children?	Er det billigere for studenter/børn?	ayr day beelēēerrer foar stoodaynterr/burrn
Have you a guide book (in English)?	Har De en brochure (på engelsk)?	haar dee ehn broashēwrer (paw ehngerlsk)
Can I buy a catalogue?	Kan jeg købe et katalog?	kehn yigh kūrber eht kaataaloa
Is it all right to take pictures?	Må man fotografere?	maw mahn foatoagrahfāȳrer

---

| **FRI ENTRE** | ADMISSION FREE |
| **FOTOGRAFERING FORBUDT** | NO CAMERAS ALLOWED |

SIGHTSEEING

Who—What—When?

What's that building?	**Hvad er det for en bygning?**	vahdh ayr day foar ehn **bewg**neeng
Who was the...?	**Hvem var...?**	vehm vahr
architect	**arkitekten**	ahrkee**tehk**tern
artist	**kunstneren**	**koonst**nererrn
painter	**maleren**	**maa**lerrern
sculptor	**billedhuggeren**	**beel**erdh**hoog**gerrern
Who painted that picture?	**Hvem har malet det billede?**	vehm haar **maa**lert day **beel**erdher
When did he live?	**Hvornår levede han?**	vornawr leh°°erdher hahn
When was it built?	**Hvornår blev det bygget?**	vornawr bleh°° day **bewg**gert
Where's the house where...lived?	**Hvor er det hus, hvor...boede?**	vōar ayr day hōōss vōar ...**bo**aerdher
We're interested in...	**Vi er interesseret i...**	vee ayr interrehss**ay**rert ee
antiques	**antikviteter**	ahnteekveet**ay**derr
archaeology	**arkæologi**	ahrkaiolog**gee**
art	**kunst**	koonst
botany	**botanik**	botah**neek**
ceramics	**keramik**	kehrah**meek**
coins	**mønter**	**murn**terr
crafts	**kunsthåndværk**	**koonst**hawnværk
fine arts	**kunst**	koonst
folk art	**folkekunst**	**foal**kerkoonst
furniture*	**møbler**	**murb**lerr
geology	**geologi**	geholog**gee**
history	**historie**	heesto**ar**ēēer
music	**musik**	moo**sseek**
natural history	**naturhistorie**	naht**ōōr**heesto**ar**ēēer
ornithology	**ornitologi/fugleliv**	oarneetoaloa**ggee**/**fool**er-lēēv
painting	**malerier**	maaler**rēē**err
pottery	**pottemagerarbejde**	**poad**eermaaerrahrbighder
sculpture	**skulptur**	skoolpt**ōōr**
wild life	**dyreliv**	**dēw**rerlēēv
zoology	**zoologi**	soaloa**ggee**
Where's the...department?	**Hvor er afdelingen for...?**	vōar ayr **ow**dehleengern foar

Just the adjective you've been looking for...

It's...	Det er...	day ayr
amazing	**forbavsende**	for**bows**serner
awful	**rædselsfuldt**	**raids**serlsfoolt
beautiful	**smukt**	smookt
delightful	**dejligt**	**digh**leet
disappointing	**skuffende**	skoo**fer**ner
gloomy	**trist**	treest
impressive	**imponerende**	impoan**ay**rerner
interesting	**interessant**	interray**ssahnt**
overwhelming	**overvældende**	o°°errvailerner
strange	**underligt**	**oon**errleet

Religious services

The majority of Danes are Protestants (Evangelical Lutheran). Sunday services are generally held at 10 a.m. and 5 p.m. Most churches are open for visitors daily from early morning to 5 or 6 p.m. If you are interested in taking photographs, obtain permission first.

In major cities there are Catholic, Baptist and Methodist churches as well as synagogues, and Copenhagen also has an English Church. For addresses and times of services, inquire at the local tourist office or consult "This Week in..." for the particular town.

Is there a...	Er der en...	ayr dayr ehn...
near here?	**her i nærheden?**	hayr ee n**ær**hehdhern
Catholic church	**katolsk kirke**	kaa**toalsk** keerker
Protestant church	**protestantisk kirke**	proader**staan**teesk **keer**ker
synagogue	**synagoge**	sewnaag**oa**er
At what time is...?	**Hvornår er der...?**	**vornawr** ayr dayr
mass	**messe**	**mays**ser
the service	**gudstjeneste**	**goods**tyaynerster
Where can I find a...	**Hvor kan jeg finde**	v**oa**r kehn yigh finner
who speaks English?	**en...der taler engelsk?**	ehn... dayr **tail**err ehng-erlsk
priest/minister/rabbi	**katolsk præst/ præst/rabbiner**	kaa**toalsk** præst/præst/ rahb**ee**nerr

Relaxing

Cinema (movies)—Theatre

You can usually buy tickets in advance for separate performances in the cinema. These consist of a feature film, occasionally a newsreel or short documentary, and numerous commercials. All foreign films are shown with the original soundtrack and Danish subtitles. In Copenhagen many cinemas have afternoon performances. Evening shows usually begin at 7 and 9 p.m.

Theatre curtain time is about 8 p.m. Advance booking is advisable.

Have you a copy of "This Week in…"?	Har De et eksemplar af "Denne uge i…?"	haar dee eht ayksehm**plahr** ah **deh**ner **ōō**er ee
What's showing at the cinema tonight?	Hvad går der i biografen i aften?	vahdh gawr dayr ee beeoagraa**fern** ee **ah**ftern
What's playing at the…Theatre?	Hvad går der på… Teatret?	vahdh gawr dayr paw… teh**ah**trert
What sort of play is it?	Hvad slags skuespil er det?	vahdh slahgss sk**ōō**erspeel ayr day
Who's it by?	Hvem har skrevet det?	vehm haar **skreh**°°ert day
Can you recommend (a)…?	Kan De anbefale…?	kehn dee **ahn**berfaaler
good film	en god film	ehn goadh feelm
comedy	et lystspil	eht **lewst**spil
something light	noget underholdende	n**ōā**ert oonerhoalerner
drama	et drama	eht **drah**mah
musical	en musical	ehn "musical"
revue	en revy	ehn reh**vew**
thriller	en gyser	ehn **gewss**err
western	en cowboy-film	ehn **ko**boi-film
At what theatre is that new play by… being performed?	På hvilket teater går det nye stykke af…?	paw **vil**kert teh**ah**terr gawr day n**ēw**er **stewg**ger ah

Where's that new film by...being shown?	**Hvor bliver den nye film af...vist?**	vōar blēēerr dehn nēwer feelm ah...veest
Who's in it?	**Hvem spiller med?**	vehm **spee**lerr maydh
Who's playing the lead?	**Hvem spiller hoved-rollen?**	vehm **spee**lerr **hoa**erdh-roalern
Who's the director?	**Hvem er instruktør?**	vehm ayr instrook**turr**
What time does it begin/end?	**Hvornår begynder/ slutter fore-stillingen?**	vornawr ber**gew**nerr/ **sloodd**err foarer-steeleengern
What time does the first evening performance start?	**Hvornår begynder den første aften-forestilling?**	vornawr ber**gew**nerr dehn **furr**ster ahftern-foarersteeleeng
Are there any tickets for tonight?	**Er der flere billetter til i aften?**	ayr dayr **flay**rer beelay-derr til ee **ah**ftern

---

🖝	🖘
Alt er desværre udsolgt.	I'm sorry, we're sold out.
Der er kun nogle få pladser tilbage i...	There are only a few seats left in the...
parkettet	stalls (orchestra)
galleriet	circle (balcony)
Der er kun ståpladser.	There's standing room only.
Må jeg se Deres billet?	May I see your ticket?

RELAXING

How much are the tickets?	**Hvad koster billetterne?**	vahdh **koast**err bee**lay**derner
I want to reserve 2 tickets for the show on Friday evening.	**Jeg vil gerne reservere 2 billetter til forestillingen fredag aften.**	yigh veel **geh**rner rayssehrv**āy**rer 2 beelayderr til foarersteeleengern **fray**dai **ah**ftern
Can I have a ticket for the matinée on Tuesday?	**Kan jeg få en billet til eftermiddags-forestillingen på tirsdag?**	kehn yigh faw ehn bee**layt** til **eh**fterrmeedaiss-foarersteeleengern paw **teers**dai
I'd like a box for 4.	**Jeg vil gerne have en loge til 4.**	yigh veel **geh**rner hæ ehn **loa**sher til 4

I want a seat in the stalls (orchestra).	**Jeg ønsker en parketplads.**	yigh **urn**skerr ehn pahr**keht**plahss
Not too far back.	**Ikke for langt tilbage.**	**igg**er foar lahngt til**baa**er
Somewhere in the middle.	**Et sted i midten.**	eht staydh ee **mee**dern
How much are the seats in the circle (balcony)?	**Hvad koster pladserne på balkonen?**	vahdh **koas**terr **plahss**serr-ner paw bahl**koa**nern
May I please have a programme?	**Kan jeg få et program?**	kehn yigh faw eht proa**grahm**
Can I check this coat?	**Kan jeg give Dem min frakke?**	kehn yigh gee dehm mēēn **frahg**ger

As there will be no usher in the theatre, you will have to look
for your seat yourself. The row and the seat number are
marked on the ticket.

Opera—Ballet—Concert

Where's the opera house?	**Hvor er operaen?**	vōar ayr **oa**pehraaern
Where's the concert hall?	**Hvor er koncertsalen?**	vōar ayr koan**sayrt**saalern
What's on at the opera tonight?	**Hvad bliver der opført på operaen i aften?**	vahdh **blēē**err dayr **op**furrt paw **oa**pehraaern ee **ahf**tern
Who's singing?	**Hvem synger?**	vehm **sewng**err
Who's dancing?	**Hvem danser?**	vehm **daans**serr
What time does the programme start?	**Hvornår begynder forestillingen?**	vor**nawr** ber**gewn**nerr **foar**ersteeleengern
What orchestra is playing?	**Hvilket orkester spiller?**	**vil**kert oar**kays**terr **spee**lerr
What's on the programme?	**Hvad står der på programmet?**	vahdh stawr dayr paw proa**grahm**mert
Who's the soloist?	**Hvem er solisten?**	vehm ayr soa**lees**tern
Who's the conductor?	**Hvem er dirigenten?**	vehm ayr deeree**egg**ehntern

Nightclubs

Along with traditional nightclubs with floor variety shows and dancing, you will find simpler bars offering music, dancing, and snacks. Membership is often required for entry to discotheques, but this can usually be arranged on the spot. There are many nightspots featuring jazz, beat or folk music, where the young meet to listen and dance, drink beer and eat a light meal.

Can you recommend a good nightclub/cabaret?	Kan De anbefale en god natklub/en kabaret?	kehn dee ahnberfaaler ehn goadh nahtkloob/ehn kahbahrāy
Is there a floor show?	Er der optræden?	ayr dayr optraidhern
What time does the floor show start?	Hvornår begynder varietéprogrammet?	vornawr bergewnerr vahrēēehtāyproagrahmert
Is evening dress necessary?	Er det nødvendigt at være selskabsklædt?	ayr day nurdvayndeet aht vǟrer saylskaabsklait

And once inside...

A table for 2, please.	Et bord til 2.	eht boar til 2
My name's... I've reserved a table for 4.	Mit navn er...Jeg har reserveret et bord til 4.	meet nown ayr...yigh haar rayssehrvāyrert eht boar til 4
We haven't got a reservation.	Vi har ingen reservation.	vee haar ingern rayssehrvahsyoan

Dancing

Where can we go dancing?	Hvor kan vi gå ud at danse?	vōar kehn vee gaw ōōdh aht daannsser
Is there a discotheque in town?	Er der et diskotek her i byen?	ayr dayr eht deeskoatāyk hayr ee bēwern
There's a dance at the...	Der er bal i...	dayr ayr bahl ee
May I have this dance?	Må jeg få denne dans?	maw yigh faw dehner daanss

Do you happen to play...?

On a rainy day, this page may solve your problems:

Do you happen to play chess?	**Spiller de tilfældigvis skak?**	speelerr dee tilfaildeevēēss skahk
Yes, I'd love to.	**Ja, meget gerne.**	yǣ mighert gehrner
I'm afraid I don't.	**Nej, det gør jeg desværre ikke.**	nigh day gurr yigh dayssvǣrer igger
No, but I'll give you a game of draughts (checkers).	**Nej, men jeg vil gerne spille dam med Dem.**	nigh mayn yigh veel gehrner speeler dahm maydh dehm
king	**konge**	koanger
queeen	**dronning**	droaneeng
castle (rook)	**tårn**	tawrn
bishop	**løber**	lurberr
knight	**springer**	spreengerr
pawn	**bonde**	boaner
Check!	**Skak!**	skahk
Checkmate!	**Skakmat!**	skahkmaht
Do you play cards?	**Spiller De kort?**	speelerr dee koart
bridge	**bridge**	"bridge"
canasta	**canasta**	kahnahstah
gin rummy	**rommy**	roamee
whist	**whist**	veest
pontoon (21)	**enogtyve**	ehnotēwver
poker	**poker**	poaggerr
ace	**es**	ayss
king	**konge**	koanger
queen	**dame**	daamer
jack	**knægt**	knehgt
joker	**joker**	yoaggerr
hearts/diamonds	**hjerter/ruder**	yayrterr/roodherr
clubs/spades	**klør/spar**	klurr/spahr

Casino and gambling

Denmark's only gambling casino—at Hotel Marienlyst in Elsinore—is open all year round from 9 p.m. to 1 a.m. To be admitted you must be over 21. The maximum stake is ten crowns.

FOR NUMBERS, see page 175

Other ways of trying your luck:

Horse-racing *(hestevæddeløb)*. Most meetings are held on Saturdays and Sundays.

Football pools *(tipning)*. Newsstands have the forms and pay off the winners. Bets involve Danish and foreign football results.

Lottery *(lotteri)*. These are run by charities or by promoters encouraging the sales of consumer goods.

Sports

If you want an active holiday, here are some popular pursuits in the great outdoors.

Cycling

Bicycles can be hired at railway stations by the hour or day. You can organize a cycling holiday through the tourist office or a travel agency. Individual arrangements provide for a 25 km (15 miles) per day itinerary, with board and lodging along the country roads you choose for your route.

Can I hire a bicycle here?	**Kan jeg leje en cykel her?**	kehn yigh **ligh**er ehn **sewgg**erl hayr
How much is it a day?	**Hvad koster det pr. dag?**	vahdh **koast**err day pehr dai
May I give the bicycle in at the end of the route in...?	**Kan jeg aflevere cyklen, når ruten er færdig i...?**	kehn yigh **ow**lehvehrer **sewgg**lern nawr **rōō**dern ayr **fæ**rdee ee

Walking

Walking holidays in the country are arranged for hikers.

Can you recommend a 3 days' route for hikers?	**Kan De anbefale en 3-dages rute til fods?**	kehn dee **ahn**berfaaler ehn 3-**dai**erss **rōō**der til foass
Where can I hire...?	**Hvor kan jeg leje...?**	vōar kehn yigh **ligh**er
rucksack	**en rygsæk**	ehn **rewg**sehk
hiking shoes	**vandresko**	**vahndr**erskoa
hiking equipment	**vandreudstyr**	**vahndr**erōōdhstewr

RELAXING

Riding

Horses may be hired at riding schools throughout the country. Many country inns also rent horses to their guests. "Riding Centres" offer all-in holidays arranged around this sport.

Where is the nearest riding school?	**Hvor er den nærmeste rideskole?**	vōār ayr dehn **nǣr**merster **rēēd**herskoaler
Can I hire a horse here?	**Kan jeg leje en hest her?**	kehn yigh **ligh**er ehn hayst hayr
How much is it per day/hour?	**Hvad koster det pr. dag/i timen?**	vahdh **koas**terr day pehr dai/ee **tēē**mern
Are there excursions with guide?	**Er der rideture med fører?**	ayr dayr **rēēd**hertōōrer maydh **furr**err
Where's the nearest race course?	**Hvor er den nærmeste hestevæddeløbsbane?**	vōār ayr dehn **nǣr**merster **hays**tervaidherlūrbsbaaner
What's the admission charge?	**Hvad koster det i entré?**	vahdh **koas**terr day ee ahntrāy
Where can I hire...?	**Hvor kan jeg leje...?**	vōār kehn yigh **ligh**er
riding boots	**ridestøvler**	**rēēd**hersturºolerr
riding equipment	**rideudstyr**	**rēēd**herōōdhstewr

Sailing

Canoes and kayaks may be hired on rivers and lakes. In most harbours motor-cruisers and sailing boats are for hire. Ask the tourist office for information on local waters.

Races and regattas are often held in summer.

Where can I hire a...?	**Hvor kan jeg leje en...?**	vōār kehn yigh **ligh**er ehn
canoe	**kano**	**kaa**noo
kayak	**kajak**	**kaa**yahk
motor boat	**motorbåd**	**mōā**toarbawdh
rowing boat	**robåd**	**roa**bawdh
sailing boat	**sejlbåd**	**sighl**bawdh
What's the charge per hour?	**Hvad koster det i timen?**	vahdh **koas**terr day ee **tēē**mern

Fishing

With its rivers, lakes and sea, Denmark is an attractive country for fishermen. Ask your local tourist office for information and any necessary permits.

How will the weather be tomorrow?	**Hvordan bliver vejret i morgen?**	vordahn bleeerr vayrert ee mōāern
Can you take us with you fishing tomorrow?	**Kan De tage os med på fisketur i morgen?**	kehn dee tæ oss maydh paw feeskertōōr ee mōāern
What is the charge?	**Hvad koster turen?**	vahdh koasterr tōōrern
When do you leave?	**Hvornår sejler De?**	vornawr sighlerr dee
Where can I hire fishing equipment?	**Hvor kan jeg leje et fiskeudstyr?**	vōār kehn yigh ligher eht feeskerōōdhstewr

On the beach

Is it safe for swimming?	**Kan man svømme uden risiko her?**	kehn mahn svurmer ōōdhern rissikoa hayr
Is there a lifeguard?	**Er der en livredder?**	ayr dayr ehn leevraydherr
Is it safe for children?	**Er det sikkert for børn?**	ayr day siggert foar burrn
There are some big waves.	**Der er store bølger.**	dayr ayr stoarer burlyerr
Is this a good place for snorkelling?	**Er det godt at dykke her?**	ayr day got aht dewgger hayr
Are there any dangerous currents?	**Er der farlig strøm?**	Ayr dayr fahrlee strurm
What time is high/low tide?	**Hvornår er det højvande/lavvande?**	vornawr ayr day hoivahner/lowvahner
What's the temperature of the water?	**Hvad er vandets temperatur?**	vahdh ayr vahnertss taympehrahrtōōr

RELAXING

PRIVAT STRAND	BADNING FORBUDT
PRIVATE BEACH	NO BATHING

I want to hire a/an/ some...	Jeg vil gerne leje...	yigh veel **gehr**ner **ligh**er
air mattress	en luftmadras	ehn **looft**mahdrahss
bath towel	et badehåndklæde	eht **baad**herhawnklaidher
bathing hut	et badehus	eht **baad**herhōōss
bathing suit	en badedragt	ehn **baad**herdrahgt
deck chair	en liggestol	ehn **ligg**erstoal
skin diving equipment	et frømandsudstyr	eht **frur**mahnssōōdhstewr
sunshade	en parasol	ehn **pah**rah**soal**
surfboard	et surf-bræt	eht **surf**-bræt
swimming belt	et svømmebælte	eht **svurm**erbehlter
tent	et telt	eht taylt
water-skis	et par vandski	eht pahr **vahn**skee

Swimming pool

Is there a swimming pool here?	Er der et svømmebassin her?	ayr dayr eht **svurm**er-baassaing hayr
Is it open-air or indoors?	Er det i fri luft eller overdækket?	ayr day ee free looft **ehl**err ō°°err**digg**ert
Is it heated?	Er det opvarmet?	ayr day **op**vahrmert

Other sports

Tennis, golf, skating and gymnastics are popular in Denmark. Every weekend there are football matches.

Is there a bowling alley near here?	Er der en bowling-bane her i nærheden?	ayr dayr ehn **bow**lingbaaner hayr ee **nær**hehdhern
I'd like to see a boxing/wrestling match.	Jeg vil gerne til en boksekamp/brydekamp.	yigh veel **gehr**ner til ehn **boaks**erkahmp/**brewdher**kahmp
Where is there a football match this weekend?	Hvor er der en fodboldkamp i weekenden?	vōar ayr dayr ehn **foadh**boalkahmp ee **week**endern
Where can I hire...?	Hvor kan jeg leje...?	vōar kehn yigh **ligh**er
golf equipment	golfudstyr	**golf**ōōdhstewr
ice skates	kunstskøjter	**koonst**skoiterr
rackets	ketsjere	**keh**cherrer

Toys

...and while the grown-ups are at play, let's not forget the children:

I'd like a/an/some...	**Jeg vil gerne have...**	yigh veel **gehr**ner hæ
badminton rackets	**nogle badminton-ketsjere**	n**ōā**ler bahd**meen**toan-**kehch**errer
beach ball	**en badebold**	ehn **baad**herboald
bicycle	**en cykel**	ehn **sewg**gerl
breathing pipe	**en snorkel**	ehn **snoar**kehl
bubble pipe	**en pibe til sæbe-bobler**	ehn **pēē**ber til **sæb**er-**boabl**errr
(plastic) bucket	**en (plastic)spand**	ehn (**plahs**tik)spahn
colouring book	**en malebog**	ehn **maal**erb**ō̄ā**
doll	**en dukke**	ehn **doog**ger
drum	**en tromme**	ehn **troam**er
flippers	**et par svømme-fødder**	eht pahr **svur**merfurdherr
floating animal	**et badedyr**	eht **baad**herd**ew̄r**
football (Br.)	**en fodbold**	ehn **foadh**boald
handball	**en håndbold**	ehn **hawn**boald
inflatable boat	**en båd til at puste op**	ehn **bawdh** til aht **poost**er op
jigsaw puzzle	**et puslespil**	eht **poos**lerspeel
jump rope	**et sjippetov**	eht **shib**bertoav
kite	**en drage**	ehn **draa**er
marbles	**nogle marmorkugler**	n**ōā**ler mahr**moar**k**ōō**lerr
model aeroplane	**en modelflyver**	ehn **moa**dayl**fl**ew̄err
paintbox	**en farvelade**	ehn **fahr**velaadher
rattle	**en rangle**	ehn **rahng**ler
roller skates	**et par rulleskøjter**	eht pahr **rol**erskoiderr
sand-box toys	**noget til sandkassen**	n**ōā**ert til **saan**kassern
skipping rope	**et sjippetov**	eht **shib**bertoav
slingshot	**en slangebøsse**	ehn **slahng**erbursser
snorkel tube	**en snorkel**	ehn **snoar**kerl
soccer ball	**en fodbold**	ehn **foadh**boald
spade	**en spade**	ehn **spaadh**er
swimming belt	**et svømmebælte**	eht **svur**merbehlter
table-tennis paddles	**et par bordtennis-bats**	eht pahr **boart**ehnisbahts
teddy bear	**en teddybjørn**	ehn **teh**dibyurrn
toy boat	**en legetøjsbåd**	ehn **ligh**ertoissbawdh
toy car	**en legetøjsbil**	ehn **ligh**ertoissb**ēē**l
water pistol	**en vandpistol**	ehn **vahn**peestoal
yoyo	**en yo-yo**	ehn yoyo

Camping—Countryside

Camping sites, many with excellent facilities, are found in various regions; a list of the locations may be obtained from any bookseller's. You need a Danish or international camping pass to use a site, though an emergency pass is issued in case of need. If you can't find a camping site and wish to use private land, be sure to get permission from the landowner.

Can we camp here?	**Må vi campere her?**	maw vee kahm**pay**rer hayr
Where can one camp for the night?	**Hvor kan man campere natten over?**	voar kehn mahn kahm**pay**rer **nah**dern o°°err
Is there a camping site near here?	**Er der en campingplads i nærheden?**	ayr dayr ehn **kahm**peengplahss ee **nær**hehdhern
May we camp in your field?	**Må vi kampere på Deres mark?**	maw vee kahm**pay**rer paw **day**rerss mahrk
Can we park our caravan (trailer) here?	**Kan vi parkere campingvognen her?**	kehn vee pahr**kay**rer **kahm**peengvoanern hayr
Is this an official camping site?	**Er dette en offentlig campingplads?**	ayr **deh**der ehn **oa**ferntlee **kahm**peengplahss
May we light a fire?	**Må vi tænde bål?**	maw vee **tain**er bawl
Is drinking water available?	**Er der drikkevand?**	ayr dayr **drig**gervahn
Are there shopping facilities on the site?	**Kan man gøre indkøb på campingpladsen?**	kehn mahn **gur**rer ink**ürb** paw **kahm**peengplahssern
Are there...?	**Er der...?**	ayr dayr
baths	**bad**	baadh
showers	**bruser**	br**oo**sserr
toilets	**toilet**	toaee**layt**

DRIKKEVAND DRINKING WATER	**FORURENET VAND** POLLUTED WATER

What's the charge?	**Hvad koster det?**	vahdh **koast**err day
per day	**pr. dag**	pehr dai
per person	**pr. person**	pehr pehr**sōān**
for a car	**for en bil**	foar ehn bēēl
for a tent	**for et telt**	foar eht taylt
for a caravan (trailer)	**for en campingvogn**	foar ehn **kahm**peengvoan
Is there a youth hostel near here?	**Er der et vandrer-hjem i nærheden?**	ayr dayr eht **vahn**drehryaym ee **næ̃r**hehdhern
Do you know anyone who can put us up for the night?	**Kender De nogen, der har plads til os natten over?**	**kay**nerr dee **nōā**ern dayr haar plahss til oss **nah**dern o°°err

CAMPERING FORBUDT NO CAMPING	CAMPINGVOGNE FRABEDES NO CARAVANS (TRAILERS)

CAMPING—COUNTRYSIDE

Landmarks

barn	**en lade**	ehn **laad**her
boulder	**en kampesten**	ehn **kahm**perstehn
bridge	**en bro**	ehn broa
building	**en bygning**	ehn **bewg**neeng
canal	**en kanal**	ehn kah**naal**
castle	**et slot**	eht sloat
chapel	**et kapel**	eht kah**payl**
church	**en kirke**	ehn **keer**ker
cliff	**en klint**	ehn kleent
copse	**et krat**	eht kraht
cottage	**en hytte**	ehn **hew**der
crossroads	**et vejkryds**	eht **vigh**krewss
farm	**en gård**	ehn gawr
ferry	**en færge**	ehn **fær**yer
field	**en mark**	ehn mahrk
forest	**en skov**	ehn sko°°
fork in the road	**en vejgaffel**	ehn **vigh**gahferl
gorge	**en slugt**	ehn sloogt
hamlet	**en lille landsby**	ehn **leel**er **lahns**bew
heath	**en hede**	ehn **heh**dher
hill	**en bakke**	ehn **bahg**ger
house	**et hus**	eht hōōss

inn	en kro	ehn kroa
lake	en sø	ehn sūr
marsh	en marsk	ehn mahrsk
moorland	en hede	ehn hehdher
path	en sti	ehn stee
peak	en top	ehn toap
pond	et kær	eht kær
pool	en dam	ehn dahm
railway	en jernbane	ehn yayrnbaaner
ravine	en kløft	ehn klurft
river	en flod	ehn floadh
road	en vej	ehn vigh
ruin	en ruin	ehn rooeēn
sea	et hav	eht how
spring	en kilde	ehn keeler
stream	en å	ehn aw
swamp	en sump	ehn soom
tower	et tårn	eht tawrn
track	et spor	eht spoar
tree	et træ	eht trai
tunnel	en tunnel	ehn toonerl
valley	en dal	ehn dahl
village	en landsby	ehn lahnsbew
waterfall	et vandfald	eht vahnfahl
well	en brønd	ehn brurn
windmill	en vindmølle	ehn vinmurler
wood	en skov	ehn sko°°

INGEN ADGANG
NO TRESPASSING

| What's the name of that stream? | **Hvad hedder den å?** | vahdh hehdherr dehn aw |
| How high is that hill? | **Hvor høj er den bakke?** | vōār hoi ayr dehn bahgger |

...and if you're tired of walking, you can always try hitch-hiking—though you may have to wait a long time for a lift.

| Can you give me a lift to...? | **Kan De tage mig med til...?** | kehn dee tæ migh maydh til |

FOR ASKING THE WAY, see also page 144

Making friends

You'll find it easy to strike up a conversation with the Danes, who are accustomed to meeting foreigners and eager to help. You'll find them hospitable as well as curious about your country.

The "Meet the Danes" programme, started by the Danish Tourist Council, permits you to visit a Danish family at home to see the way of life and discuss subjects of mutual interest. You have to go to a tourist information office 48 hours in advance to arrange this free programme. It operates in the following cities: Copenhagen, Aarhus, Aalborg, Esbjerg, Fredericia, Herning, Horsens, Kolding, Odense, Silkeborg, Skanderborg, Skive, Slagelse and Vejle.

Introductions

How are you?	**Hvordan har De det?**	vordahn haar dee day
Fine, thanks. And you?	**Tak, godt. Og De?**	tæk got oa dee
My name's...	**Mit navn er...**	meet nown ayr
Glad to know you.	**Det glæder mig at træffe Dem.**	day **glaidh**err migh aht **trehf**er dehm

Follow-up

How long have you been here?	**Hvor længe har De været her?**	voar **lain**ger haar dee **vǣ**rert hayr
We've been here a week.	**Vi har været her en uge.**	vee haar **vǣ**rert hayr ehn **ōō**er
Is this your first visit?	**Er det første gang, De er her?**	ayr day **furr**ster gahng dee ayr hayr
No, we came here last year.	**Nej, vi var her også sidste år.**	nigh vee vaar hayr **oss**aw **seest**er awr
Are you enjoying your stay?	**Kan De lide at være her?**	kehn dee **lǣ**dher aht **vǣ**rer hayr
Yes, I like... very much.	**Ja, jeg synes vældig godt om...**	yæ yigh **sēw**nerss **vail**dee got oam

Are you on your own?	Rejser De alene?	righsserr dee aalāyner
I'm with...	Jeg er her sammen med...	yigh ayr hayr sahmern maydh
my husband	min mand	mēēn mahn
my wife	min kone	mēēn koaner
my family	min familie	mēēn fahmēēlēēer
my parents	mine forældre	mēēner forehldrer
some friends	nogle venner	nōaler vaynerr
Where do you come from?	Hvor kommer De fra?	vōar koamerr dee fraa
I'm from...	Jeg kommer fra...	yigh koamerr fraa
Where are you staying?	Hvor bor De?	vōar bōar dee
I'm a student.	Jeg er studerende.	yigh ayr stoodāyrerner
We're here on holiday.	Vi er her på ferie.	vee ayr hayr paw fehrēēer
I'm here on business.	Jeg er her på forretningsrejse.	yigh ayr hayr paw forraytneengsrighsser
I hope we'll see you again soon.	Jeg håber, vi snart ses igen.	yigh hawberr vee snahrt sāys eeggayn
See you later/See you tomorrow.	På gensyn/Vi ses i morgen.	paw gehnsewn/vee sāys ee mōaern

The weather

Always a good topic for conversation, in Denmark as elsewhere.

What a lovely day!	Hvor er det et dejligt vejr i dag!	vōar ayr day eht dighleet vayr ee dai
What awful weather!	Sikke et skrækkeligt vejr!	sigger eht skrehggerleet vayr
Isn't it cold/hot today?	Er det ikke koldt/varmt i dag?	ayr day igger kolt/vahrmt ee dai
Do you think it'll... tomorrow?	Tror De, det... i morgen?	troar dee day...ee mōaern
rain/snow	regner/sner	righnerr/snehr
clear up/be sunny	klarer op/bliver solskinsvejr	klahrerr op/blēēerr soalskeensvayr
What's the weather forecast?	Hvad siger vejrmeldingen?	vahdh sēēerr vayrmayleengern

Invitations

My wife and I would like you to dine with us on...	**Min kone og jeg vil gerne invitere Dem* til middag på...**	mēēn koaner oa yigh veel gehrner inveetāyrer dehm til midai paw
Can you come to dinner tomorrow night?	**Kan De* komme til middag i morgen aften?**	kehn dee koamer til midai ee mōāern ahftern
Can you join us for a drink this evening?	**Kan De komme i aften til en drink?**	kehn dee koamer ee ahftern til ehn drink
There's a party. Are you coming?	**Der skal være selskab. Kommer De?**	dayr skahl væērer saylskahb. koamerr dee
That's very kind of you.	**Det er meget venligt af Dem.**	day ayr mighert vaynleet ah dehm
Great. I'd love to come.	**Storartet. Jeg vil meget gerne komme.**	stoarahrtert. yigh veel mighert gehrner koamer
What time shall we come?	**Hvad tid skal vi komme?**	vahdh teedh skahl vee koamer
May I bring a friend?	**Må jeg tage en bekendt med?**	maw yigh tæ ehn behkaynt maydh
I'm afraid we've got to go now.	**Vi bliver desværre nødt til at gå nu.**	vee blēēerr dayssvæērer nurdh til aht gaw noo
Next time you must come to visit us.	**Næste gang må De besøge os.**	nehster gahng maw dee bersurer oss
Thanks for the evening. It was great.	**Tusind tak for den dejlige aften.**	tōōsseen tæk foar dehn dighlēēer ahftern

Dating

Would you like a cigarette?	**Må jeg byde Dem en cigaret?**	maw yigh bēwdher dehm ehn siggahrayt
Do you have a light, please?	**Undskyld, har De ild?**	oonskewl haar dee eel
Can I get you a drink?	**Må jeg byde Dem en drink?**	maw yigh bēwdher dehm ehn drink
Excuse me, could you please help me?	**Undskyld, vil De gøre mig en tjeneste.**	oonskewl veel dee gūrrer migh ehn tyaynerster

* For ease of reading we give only the formal second person form of address (**De/Dem**) here. The more informal or intimate **du/dig** can be used under certain circumstances only.

I'm lost. Can you show me the way to…?	Jeg er faret vild. Kan De vise mig vejen til…?	yigh ayr **faa**rert veel. kehn dee **vee**sser migh **vigh**ern til
Are you free this evening?	Er De ledig i aften?	ayr dee **leh**dhee ee **ah**ftern
Would you like to go out with me tonight?	Har De lyst til at gå ud med mig i aften?	haar dee lewst til aht gaw ōōdh maydh migh ee **ah**ftern
Would you like to go dancing?	Skal vi tage ud at danse?	skahl vee tæ ōōdh aht **daan**sser
I know a good disco-theque/restaurant.	Jeg kender et godt diskotek/en god restaurant.	yigh **keh**nerr eht got deeskoa**tayk**/ehn goadh raystoa**rahng**
Shall we go to the cinema (movies)?	Skal vi gå i biografen?	skahl vee gaw ee beeoa**graa**fern
Would you like to go for a drive?	Har De lyst til at køre en tur?	haar dee lewst til aht **kūr**rer ehn tōōr
I'd love to, thank you.	Tak, det vil jeg gerne.	tæk day veel yigh **geh**rner
Where shall we meet?	Hvor skal vi mødes?	vōar skahl vee **mūr**dherss
I'll pick you up at your hotel.	Jeg henter Dem på hotellet.	yigh **hay**nterr dehm paw hoa**tay**lert
I'll call for you at 8.	Jeg henter Dem klokken 8.	yigh **hay**nterr dehm **kloa**ggern 8
May I take you home?	Må jeg følge Dem hjem?	maw yigh **fur**lyerr dehm yaym
Can I see you again tomorrow?	Kan vi mødes igen i morgen?	kehn vee **mūr**dherss eeg**ayn** ee **mōa**ern
Thank you, it's been a wonderful evening.	Tak. Det har været en dejlig aften.	tæk. day haar **væ**rert ehn **digh**lee **ah**ftern
What's your telephone number?	Hvad er Deres* telefonnummer?	vahdh ayr **day**rerss tehler-**fōa**noommerr
Do you live with your family?	Bor De hos Deres** familie?	bōar dee hoass **day**rerss fah**mee**leeer
What time is your last bus?	Hvornår går Deres** sidste bus?	vor**nawr** gawr **day**rerss **sees**ter booss

* Informally, **Deres** here becomes **dit** (deet).
Informally, **Deres here becomes **din** (dēēn).

Shopping guide

This shopping guide is designed to help you find what you want with ease, accuracy and speed. It features:

1. A list of all major types of shops and services (page 98)
2. Some general expressions required when shopping to allow you to define your requirements precisely when asking for an article (page 100)
3. Full details of the shops and services likely to concern you. Here you'll find advice, phrases, alphabetical lists of items and conversion charts listed under the headings below.

		Page
Bookshop	reading matter, stationery, authors	104
Camping	camping equipment, crockery, cutlery	106
Chemist's (drugstore)	medicine, first-aid, toilet articles	108
Clothing	clothes, shoes, accessories, material, colours, clothing sizes	112
Electrical appliances	radio & TV, records, recording artists, razors, repairs	119
Hairdresser's	barber's, ladies' hairdresser's	121
Jeweller's	watches, repairs, jewellery	123
Laundry— Dry-cleaning	usual facilities	126
Photography	film, processing, accessories, repairs	127
Provisions	what you'll want to buy for a picnic	130
Souvenirs	souvenirs, gifts	132
Tobacconist's	smoker's supplies	133

SHOPPING GUIDE

Shops, stores and services

Shopping hours: Generally 9 or 9.30 a.m. to 5.30 p.m., Monday to Thursday. Latenight shopping extends to 7 or 8 p.m. on Fridays, and sometimes on Thursdays also. Saturday is early closing day at 1 or 2 p.m.

In Copenhagen and a few other cities, several shops open part of the day on Sundays, usually in the morning— bakers', florists', *smørrebrød* shops, sweet shops and kiosks.

Note: Some shops (often food) are closed on Monday or Tuesday.

Were's the nearest...?	Hvor er nærmeste...?	vōār ayr nǣrmerster
antique shop	antikvitetsforretning	ahnteekveetāȳtsforraytneeng
art gallery	kunstgallerj	koonstgahlerree
bakery	bageri	baaerree
bank	bank	bahnk
barber	barber	bahrbāȳr
beauty salon	skønhedssalon	skurnhaydhssahlong
bookshop	boghandel	bōāhahnerl
butcher	slagter	slahgterr
camera store	fotoforretning	foatoaforraytneeng
candy store	chokoladeforretning	shoakoalaadherforraytneeng
chemist's	apotek	ahpoatāȳk
cigarette stand	kiosk	kyoask
cobbler	skomager	skoamaaerr
confectioner	konditori	koandeetoaree
dairy	mælkeudsalg	mehlkerōōdhsaal
delicatessen	viktualiehandler	veektooaalēēerhahnlerr
dentist	tandlæge	tahnlaier
department store	stormagasin	stoarmahgahsēēn
doctor	læge	laier
draper	manufakturhandler	maanoofahktōōrhahnlerr
dressmaker	dameskrædder	daamerskrædherr
drugstore	apotek	ahpoatāȳk
dry cleaner	renseri	raynsserree
dry-goods store	manufakturhandel	maanoofahktōōrhahnerl
fishmonger	fiskehandel	feeskerhahnerl
flea market	loppemarked	loabermahrkerdh

florist	blomsterforretning	bloamsterrforraytneeng
furrier	buntmager	boontmaaerr
garage (car repairs)	bilværksted	beelværkstaydh
greengrocer	grønthandel	grurnthahnerl
grocery	købmand	kurbmahn
hairdresser (ladies)	damefrisør	daamerfreessurr
hardware store	isenkræmmer	eessernkræmerr
hat shop	hatteforretning	haaderforraytneeng
health-food shop	helsekost-forretning	haylsserkoastforrayt-neeng
ironmonger	isenkræmmer	eessernkræmerr
jeweller	guldsmed	goolsmehdh
launderette	quick-vask	"quick"-vahsk
laundry	vaskeri	vahskerree
leather-goods store	lædervarer-forretning	laidherværerforraytneeng
liquor store	vinhandel	veenhahnerl
market	marked	mahrkerdh
milliner	modeforretning	moadherforraytneeng
newsagent	bladhandel	blahdhhahnerl
optician	optiker	oaptiggerr
pastry shop	konditori	koandeetoaree
pawnbroker	pantelåner	paanterlawnerr
photo shop	fotoforretning	foatoaforraytneeng
post office	posthus	poasthooss
shirt-maker	skjorteforretning	skyoarterforraytneeng
shoemaker (repairs)	skomager	skoamaaerr
shoe shop	skoforretning	skoaforraytneeng
silversmith	sølvsmed	surlsmehdh
souvenir shop	souvenirforretning	sooverneerforraytneeng
sporting-goods shop	sportsforretning	spoartsforraytneeng
stationer	papirhandel	pahpeerhahnerl
supermarket	supermarked	sooberrmahrkerdh
sweet shop	chokolade-forretning	shoakoalaadherforrayt-neeng
tailor	skrædder	skrædherr
telegraph office	telegraf	tehlergrahf
tobacconist	tobakshandel	toabahkshahnerl
toiletry shop	parfumeri	parhfewmerree
toy shop*	legetøjs-forretning	lighertoissforrayt-neeng
travel agency	rejsebureau	righssserbewroa
vegetable store	grønthandel	grurnthahnerl
watchmaker	urmager	oormaaerr

SHOPPING GUIDE

---
* see page 89

General expressions

Here are some expressions which will be useful to you when you're out shopping:

Where's a good...?	**Hvor er der en god...?**	vōar ayr dayr ehn goadh
Where can I find a...?	**Hvor findes der en...?**	vōar finnerss dayr ehn
Where do they sell...?	**Hvor sælger man...?**	vōar saylgerr mahn
Can you recommend an inexpensive...?	**Kan De anbefale en billig...?**	kehn dee ahnberfaaler ehn beelee
Where's the main shopping area?	**Hvor er forretnings-kvarteret?**	vōar ayr forraytneengs-kvahrtayrert
How far is it from here?	**Hvor langt er det herfra?**	vōar lahngt ayr day hayrfraa
How do I get there?	**Hvordan kommer jeg dertil?**	vordahn koamerr yigh dayrtil

SÆRTILBUD SPECIAL OFFER	**BILLIGE TILBUD** BARGAIN
UDSALG SALES	

Service

Can you help me?	**Kan De hjælpe mig?**	kehn dee yehlper migh
I'm just looking around.	**Jeg kigger bare.**	yigh kiggerr baarer
I want...	**Jeg ønsker...**	yigh urnskerr
Can you show me some...?	**Kan De vise mig nogle...?**	kehn dee vēēsser migh nōaler
Do you have any...?	**Har De nogen...?**	haar dee nōaern

That one

Can you show me...?	**Kan De vise mig...?**	kehn dee vēēsser migh
that/those	**den dér/de dér**	dehn dayr/dee dayr
the one in the window	**den, der er i vinduet**	dehn dayr ayr ee veendōoert
the one in the display case	**den, der er i udhængsskabet**	dehn dayr ayr ee ōōdhhayngskaabert
It's over there.	**Den er derovre.**	dehn ayr dayrooer

FOR COLOURS, see page 113

Defining the article

I'd like a...	**Jeg vil gerne have...**	yigh veel **gehr**ner hæ
I want a... one.	**Jeg ønsker en...**	yigh **urn**skerr ehn
big	**stor**	stoar
cheap	**billig**	**bee**lee
coloured	**farvet**	**fahr**vert
dark	**mørk**	murrk
hard	**hård**	hawr
heavy	**tung**	toong
large	**stor**	stoar
light (weight)	**let**	leht
light (colour)	**lys**	lewss
long	**lang**	lahng
modern	**moderne**	moa**day**rner
oval	**oval**	oa**vaal**
rectangular	**rektangulær**	raytahng**goo**lær
round	**rund**	roon
short	**kort**	koart
small	**lille**	**lee**ler
soft	**blød**	blurdh
square	**firkantet**	**feer**kaantert
sturdy	**robust**	roa**boost**
I don't want anything too expensive.	**Jeg vil ikke have noget, der er for dyrt.**	yigh veel **igg**er hæ **nōā**ert dayr ayr foar dewrt

Preference

Can you show me some more?	**Kan De vise mig nogle andre?**	kehn dee **vēē**sser migh **nōā**ler **ahn**drer
Haven't you anything...?	**Har De ikke noget...?**	haar dee **igg**er **nōā**ert
cheaper/better	**billigere/bedre**	beel**ēē**errer/**bay**dhrer
larger/smaller	**større/mindre**	**stur**rer/**min**drer

How much?

How much is it?	**Hvad koster det?**	vahdh **koast**err day
I don't understand.	**Det forstår jeg ikke.**	day for**staw**r yigh **igg**er
Please write it down.	**Vær venlig at skrive det ned.**	vær **vehn**lee aht **skrēē**ver day naydh
I don't want to spend more than... crowns.	**Det må ikke koste mere end... kroner.**	day maw **igg**er **koast**er **māy**rer ehn... **krōā**nerr

Decision

That's just what I want.	**Det er lige, hvad jeg vil have.**	day ayr **lēē**er vahdh yigh veel hæ
It's not quite what I want.	**Det er ikke helt det, jeg ønsker.**	day ayr **igg**er hehlt day yigh **urn**skerr
No, I don't like it.	**Nej, det bryder jeg mig ikke om.**	nigh day **brewdh**err yigh migh **igg**er oam
I'll take it.	**Jeg tager det.**	yigh taar day

Ordering

Can you order it for me?	**Kan De bestille det til mig?**	kehn dee ber**steel**er day til migh
How long will it take?	**Hvor længe varer det?**	vōar **lainger vǣ**rerr day
I'd like it as soon as possible.	**Jeg vil gerne have den snarest muligt.**	yigh veel **gehr**ner hæ dehn **snah**rerst **mōō**leet
Will I have any difficulty with customs?	**Får jeg besvær i tolden?**	fawr yigh beh**svǣr** ee **toa**lern

Delivery

I'll take it with me.	**Jeg tager den med.**	yigh taar dehn maydh
Deliver it to the... Hotel.	**Send den til Hotel...**	sayn dehn til hoa**tayl**
Please send it to this address.	**Send den venligst til denne adresse.**	sayn dehn **vehn**leest til **deh**ner ah**dray**sser

Paying

How much is it?	**Hvor meget bliver det?**	vōar **migh**ert **blēē**err day
Can I pay by traveller's cheque?	**Kan jeg betale med rejsechecks?**	kehn yigh ber**taa**ler maydh **righ**sserchayks
Do you accept dollars/pounds/credit cards?	**Tager De imod dollars/pund/ kreditkort?**	taar dee ee**moadh** dollarss/ poon/krayd**ēē**tkoart
Haven't you made a mistake in the bill?	**Har De ikke lavet en fejl på regningen?**	haar dee **igg**er **laa**vert ehn fighl paw **righ**neengern
Can I please have a receipt?	**Må jeg få en kvittering?**	maw yigh faw ehn kveet**āy**reeng

Anything else?

No, thanks, that's all.	**Nej tak, det var det hele.**	nigh tæk day vaar day **hay**ler
Yes, I want...	**Ja, jeg vil gerne have...**	yaa yigh veel **gehr**ner hæ
Show me...	**Vis mig...**	v**ee**ss migh
Thank you. Good-bye.	**Tak. Farvel.**	tæk. fahr**vehl**

Dissatisfied

Can you please exchange this?	**Kan jeg få dette byttet?**	kehn yigh faw **deh**der **bew**dert
I want to return this.	**Jeg ønsker at levere dette tilbage.**	yigh **ur**nsker aht leh-**vay**rer **deh**der tilbaaer
I'd like a refund. Here's the receipt.	**Jeg vil gerne have det refunderet. Her er kvitteringen.**	yigh veel **gehr**ner hæ day rayfoond**ay**rert. hayr ayr kveet**ay**reengern

---

Kan jeg hjælpe Dem?	Can I help you?
Hvad ønsker De?	What would you like?
Hvilken...ønsker De?	What...would you like?
farve/form kvalitet/antal	colour/shape quality/quantity
Jeg beklager, det har vi ikke.	I'm sorry, we haven't any.
Der er udsolgt.	We're out of stock.
Skal vi bestille det til Dem?	Shall we order it for you?
Tager De den med eller skal vi sende den?	Will you take it with you or shall we send it?
Skulle der være andet?	Anything else?
Det bliver...kroner, tak.	That's...crowns, please.
Kassen er derovre.	The cashier's over there.

SHOPPING GUIDE

Bookshop—Stationer's—News-stand

In Denmark, bookshops often offer stationer's supplies, too.
British and American newspapers and magazines are sold at
news-stands in large cities and at major railway stations.

SHOPPING GUIDE

Where's the nearest...?	**Hvor er den nærmeste...?**	vōār ayr dehn **næ**rmerster
bookshop	**boghandel**	**bōā**hahnerl
stationer's	**papirhandel**	pah**pēēr**hahnerl
news-stand	**aviskiosk**	ah**vēēs**kyoask
Can you recommend a good bookshop?	**Kan De anbefale en god boghandel?**	kehn dee ahnberfaaler ehn goadh **bōā**hahnerl
Where can I buy an English newspaper?	**Hvor kan jeg købe en engelsk avis?**	vōār kehn yigh **kūr**ber ehn **ehng**erlsk ah**vēēss**
I want to buy a/an/ some...	**Jeg ønsker at købe...**	yigh **urn**skerr aht **kūr**ber
address book	**en adressebog**	ehn ah**drāy**sserbōā
ball-point pen	**en kuglepen**	ehn **kōō**lerpayn
blotting paper	**noget trækpapir**	**nōā**ert **trehk**pahpēēr
book	**en bog**	ehn bōā
carbon paper	**noget karbonpapir**	**nōā**ert **kahr**boanpahpēēr
cellophane tape	**en rulle tape**	ehn rooler taip
crayons	**nogle farveblyanter**	**nōā**ler **fahr**verblewahnterr
dictionary	**en ordbog**	ehn **oar**bōā
Danish-English	**dansk-engelsk**	dahnsk-**ehng**erlsk
English-Danish	**engelsk-dansk**	**ehng**erlsk-dahnsk
pocket dictionary	**en lommeordbog**	ehn **loam**eroarbōā
drawing paper	**noget tegnepapir**	**nōā**ert **tighn**erpahpēēr
drawing pins	**nogle tegnestifter**	**nōā**ler **tighn**ersteefterr
envelopes	**nogle konvolutter**	**nōā**ler **koan**volōōderr
eraser	**et viskelæder**	eht **vees**kerlaidherr
exercise book	**et kladdehæfte**	eht **klaad**herhehfter
file	**en brevordner**	ehn **bray**voardnerr
fountain pen	**en fyldepen**	ehn **few**lerpehn
glue	**noget lim**	**nōā**ert leem
grammar book	**en grammatik**	ehn grahmah**tēēk**
guide book	**en rejsehåndbog**	ehn **righ**sserhawnbōā
ink	**noget blæk**	**nōā**ert blehk
black/red/blue	**sort/rødt/blåt**	soart/rurt/blawt
labels	**nogle etiketter**	**nōā**ler **ehtee**kayderr
magazine	**et ugeblad**	eht **ōō**erblaadh
map	**et kort**	eht koart
map of the town	**bykort**	**bew**koart
road map of...	**vejkort over...**	**vigh**koart o°°er

newspaper	**en avis**	ehn ahv**eess**
American	**amerikansk**	ahmehree**kaansk**
English	**engelsk**	**ehng**erlsk
notebook	**en notesbog**	ehn no**aderssboa**
paperback	**en billigbog**	ehn bee**leeboa**
paper napkins	**nogle papirs-serrvietter**	n**oa**ler pah**peers-**sayrv**eee**ehderr
paste	**noget klister**	n**oa**ert **klees**terr
pen	**en pen**	ehn pehn
pencil	**en blyant**	ehn **blew**aant
pencil sharpener	**en blyantsspidser**	ehn **blew**aantspeesserr
playing cards	**et spil kort**	eht speel koart
postcards	**nogle postkort**	n**oa**ler **poast**koart
refill (for a pen)	**en patron (til fyldepen)**	ehn **paatroan** (til **few**lerpehn)
rubber	**et viskelæder**	eht **vees**kerlaidherr
ruler	**en lineal**	ehn **lee**neeahl
sketching block	**en skitseblok**	ehn **skeets**erbloak
string	**noget snor**	n**oa**ert snoar
thumbtacks	**nogle tegnestifter**	n**oa**ler **tigh**nersteeferr
tracing paper	**noget kalkérpapir**	n**oa**ert kahl**kayr**pahp**eer**
typewriter ribbon	**et farvebånd (til skrivemaskine)**	eht **fahr**verbawn (til skr**eee**vermaask**eee**ner)
typing paper	**noget skrive-maskinepapir**	n**oa**ert skr**eee**vermaask**eee**nerpahp**eer**
wrapping paper	**noget indpaknings-papir**	n**oa**ert in**pah**kneengs-pahp**eer**
writing pad	**en skriveblok**	ehn **skreee**verbloak
Where's the guide-book section?	**Hvor er afdelingen for rejsehåndbøger?**	v**oa**r ayr **ow**dehleengern foar **righss**erhawnb**u**rerr
Where do you keep the English books?	**Hvor står de engelske bøger?**	v**oa**r stawr dee **ehng**erlsker b**u**rerr
Have you any of...'s books in English?	**Har De nogen af...s bøger på engelsk?**	haar dee n**oa**ern ah...s b**u**rerr paw **ehng**erlsk
Is there an English translation of...?	**Findes der en engelsk over-sættelse af...?**	finnerss dayr ehn **ehng**erlsk o°°ersehderlsser ah

Here are some contemporary Danish authors whose books are available in English translation:

Anders Bodelsen
Cecil Bødker
Tove Ditlevsen
Piet Hein

Frank Jæger
Leif Panduro
Klaus Rifbjerg
Hans Scherfig

Camping

Here we're concerned with the equipment you may need.

I'd like a/an/some…	Jeg vil gerne have…	yigh veel **gehr**ner hæ
axe	**en økse**	ehn **urk**ser
bottle-opener	**en flaskeåbner**	ehn **flahs**kerawbnerr
bucket	**en spand**	ehn spahn
butane gas	**noget flaskegas**	**nōā**ert **flahs**kergaass
camp bed	**en drømmeseng**	ehn **drur**merssayng
camping equipment	**noget camping-udstyr**	**nōā**ert **kahm**peeng-**ōōdh**stewr
can opener	**en dåseåbner**	ehn **daws**serawbnerr
candles	**nogle stearinlys**	**nōā**ler stayar**ēēn**lewss
chair	**en stol**	ehn stoal
folding chair	**en klapstol**	ehn **klahp**stoal
compass	**et kompas**	eht **koam**pahss
corkscrew	**en proptrækker**	ehn **proap**trehggerr
crockery	**noget porcelæn**	**nōā**ert **poars**serlain
cutlery	**et spisebestik**	eht **spēē**sserbersteek
deck-chair	**en liggestol**	ehn **ligger**stoal
first-aid kit	**en nødhjælpskasse**	ehn **nurdh**yehlpskaasser
fishing tackle	**nogle fiskegrejer**	**nōā**ler feeskergrigherr
flashlight	**en lommelygte**	ehn **loamer**lewgter
frying-pan	**en stegepande**	ehn **sti**gherpaaner
groundsheet	**et teltunderlag**	eht **tay**ltoonerrlaa
hammer	**en hammer**	ehn **hah**merr
hammock	**en hængekøje**	ehn **hai**ngerkoier
haversack	**en skuldertaske**	ehn **skoo**lerrtaasker
ice bag	**en ispose**	ehn **ēēss**poasser
kerosene	**noget petroleum**	**nōā**ert pehtr**ōā**lehoom
kettle	**en kedel**	ehn **keh**dherl
knapsack	**en rygsæk**	ehn **rewg**sehk
lamp	**en lampe**	ehn **lah**mper
lantern	**en lygte**	ehn **lewg**ter
matches	**nogle tændstikker**	**nōā**ler tainstiggerr
mattress	**en madras**	ehn **maa**drahss
methylated spirits	**noget denatureret sprit**	**nōā**ert dehnaatoorr**āy**rert spreet
mosquito net	**et moskitonet**	eht moask**ēē**toanayt
pail	**en spand**	ehn spahn
paraffin	**noget petroleum**	**nōā**ert pehtr**ōā**lehoom
penknife	**en lommekniv**	ehn **loamer**kn**ēē**v
picnic case	**en picnic-kuffert**	ehn **pik**nik-**koo**ffert
pressure cooker	**en trykkoger**	ehn **trewk**koaerr
primus stove	**en primus**	ehn **prēē**mooss
rope	**et reb**	eht rayb

rucksack	en rygsæk	ehn rewgsehk
saucepan	en kasserolle	ehn kahsseroāler
scissors	en saks	ehn sahks
screwdriver	en skruetrækker	ehn skrōōertrehggerr
sheathknife	en dolk	ehn dolk
sleeping bag	en sovepose	ehn so°°erpoasser
stewpan	en stegegryde	ehn stighergrēwdher
stove	et komfur	eht koamfōōr
table	et bord	eht boar
folding table	et klapbord	eht klahpboar
tent	et telt	eht taylt
tent pegs	nogle teltpløkke	nōāler tayltplewggerr
tent pole	en teltstang	ehn tayltstahng
thermos flask (bottle)	en termoflaske	ehn tehrmoaflahsker
tin opener	en dåseåbner	ehn dawsserawbnerr
tongs	en tang	ehn tahng
tool kit	et værktøjssæt	eht værktoisseht
torch	en lommelygte	ehn loamerlewgter
wood alcohol	noget kogesprit	nōāert koaerspreet

Crockery

cups	kopper	koaberr
dishes	fade	faadher
food box	madkasse	mahdhkaasser
mugs	krus	krōōss
plates	tallerkener	tahlāyrkernerr
saucers	underkopper	oonerkoaberr

Cutlery

forks	gafler	gahflerr
knives	knive	knēēver
spoons	skeer	skeherr
teaspoons	teskeer	tehskeherr
(made of) plastic	af plastic	ah plahstik
(made of) stainless steel	af rustfrit stål	ah roostfreet stawl

Chemist's (Drugstore)

A Danish *apotek* doesn't normally stock the great range of goods you find in the equivalent chemist's shop in Britain or, especially, in a U.S. drugstore. For example, it doesn't sell photographic equipment or books. For perfume and cosmetics there are separate shops, *parfumeri*.

To find an all-night chemist's, consult the notice in the window of any chemist's shop.

This section has been divided into two parts:

1. Pharmaceutical—medicine, first-aid etc.
2. Toiletry—toilet articles, cosmetics

General

Where's the nearest (all-night) chemist's?	**Hvor er det nærmeste (nat)apotek?**	vōar ayr day nǣrmerster (naht)ahpoatāyk
What time does the chemist's open/close?	**Hvornår åbner/lukker apoteket?**	vornawr awbnerr/looggerr ahpoatāykert

Part 1—Pharmaceutical

I want something for...	**Jeg vil gerne have noget mod...**	yigh veel gehrner hæ nōaert moadh
a cold/a cough	**forkølelse/hoste**	forkūrlerlsser/hoaster
hay fever	**høfeber**	hurfehberr
a hangover	**tømmermænd**	turmerrmehn
sunburn	**solforbrænding**	soalforbrehneeng
travel sickness	**køresyge**	kūrrersēwer
an upset stomach	**dårlig mave**	dawrlee maaver
Can you make up this prescription for me?	**Kan De give mig, hvad der står på denne recept?**	kehn dee gee migh vahdh dayr stawr paw dehner rehsehpt
Shall I wait?	**Skal jeg vente?**	skahl yigh vaynter
When shall I come back?	**Hvornår kan jeg komme tilbage?**	vornawr kehn yigh koamer tilbaaer
Can I get it without a prescription?	**Kan jeg få det uden recept?**	kehn yigh faw day ōodhern rehsehpt

FOR DOCTOR, see page 162

Can I have a/an/ some...?	**Kan jeg få...?**	kehn yigh faw
ammonia	**noget ammoniak**	nōaert ahmoaneeahk
antiseptic cream	**en antiseptisk creme**	ehn ahnteesaypteesk kraym
aspirin	**en æske aspirin**	ehn ehsker ahspeerēēn
bandage	**en bandage**	ehn baandaasher
Band-Aids	**noget hæfteplaster**	nōaert hehfterplahsterr
calcium tablets	**nogle kalktabletter**	nōaler kahlktahblayderr
chlorine tablets	**nogle klortabletter**	nōaler kloartahblayderr
contraceptives	**et antikonceptions- middel**	eht ahnteekoansayp- syoansmeederl
corn plasters	**et ligtorneplaster**	eht lēētoarnerplahsterr
cotton wool	**noget vat**	nōaert vaht
cough mixture	**noget hostesaft**	nōaert hoastersahft
diabetic lozenges	**nogle insulinpiller**	nōaler insoolēēnpeelerr
disinfectant	**et desinfektions- middel**	eht dehseenfayksyoans meederl
ear drops	**nogle øredråber**	nōaler ūrrerdrawberr
first-aid kit	**en nødhjælpskasse**	ehn nurdhyehlpskaasser
gargle	**en flaske gurglevand**	ehn flahsker goorlervahn
gauze	**noget gaze**	nōaert gaasser
insect lotion	**en insektcreme**	ehn insehktkraym
iodine	**noget jod**	nōaert yoadh
iron pills	**nogle jernpiller**	nōaler yayrnpeelerr
laxative	**et afføringsmiddel**	eht owfurreengsmeederl
mouthwash	**noget mundvand**	nōaert moonvahn
quinine tablets	**nogle kininpiller**	nōaler keenēēnpeelerr
sanitary napkins	**nogle hygiejnebind**	nōaler hewgeeyehnerbeen
sedative	**et beroligende middel**	eht behroalēēerner mee- dherl
sleeping pills	**nogle sovepiller**	nōaler so°°erpeelerr
stomach pills	**nogle mavetabletter**	nōaler maavertahblayderr
surgical dressing	**et forbindings- linned**	eht forbeeneengsleen- nerdh
thermometer	**et termometer**	eht tehrmoamāyderr
throat lozenges	**nogle halspastiller**	nōaler hahlspaasteelerr
tonic	**et styrkende middel**	eht stewrkerner meedherl
tranquillizers	**et beroligende middel**	eht behroalēēerner mee- dherl
vitamin pills	**nogle vitaminpiller**	nōaler veetaamēēnpeelerr

---

GIFT!   POISON!
KUN TIL UDVORTES BRUG!   FOR EXTERNAL USE ONLY!

Part 2—Toiletry

I'd like a/an/some...	Jeg vil gerne have...	yigh veel **gehr**ner hæ
acne cream	en **filipenscreme**	ehn feelee**payns**kraym
after-shave lotion	en **barberlotion**	ehn bahr**bāyr**loasyoan
astringent	en **ansigtstonic**	ehn **ahns**eegtstonik
bath essence	en **badeparfume**	ehn **baad**herpahrfēwmer
cream	en **creme**	ehn kraym
cleansing cream	**rensecreme**	**rayns**erkraym
cold cream	**coldcreme**	**koal**kraym
cuticle cream	**neglebåndscreme**	**nigh**lerbawnskraym
enzyme cream	**enzymcreme**	ehn**sēwm**kraym
foundation cream	**underlagscreme**	**oon**erlaaskraym
hormone cream	**hormoncreme**	hoar**moan**kraym
moisturizing cream	**fugtighedscreme**	**foog**teehehdhskraym
night cream	**natcreme**	**naht**kraym
cuticle remover	noget **neglebånds-fjerner**	nōaert **nigh**lerbawns-fyayrnerr
deodorant	en **deodorant**	ehn de**hoa**doarahnt
emery board	en **neglefil med sandpapir**	ehn **nigh**lerfēēl maydh sahnpahpēēr
eye liner	en **eye-liner**	ehn "eye-liner"
eye pencil	en **øjenstift**	ehn **oi**ernsteeft
eye shadow	en **øjenskygge**	ehn **oi**ernskewgger
face flannel	en **vaskeklud**	ehn **vahs**kerklōōdh
face pack	en **ansigtsmaske**	ehn **ahns**eegtsmaasker
face powder	noget **ansigtspudder**	nōaert **ahns**eegtspoodherr
foot cream	en **fodcreme**	ehn **foadh**kraym
hand cream/lotion	en **håndcreme/håndlotion**	ehn **hawn**kraym/**hawn**loasyoan
lipsalve	en **læbepomade**	ehn **laib**erpoamaadher
lipstick	en **læbestift**	ehn **laib**ersteeft
lipstick brush	en **læbestift-pensel**	ehn **laib**ersteeft-paynsserl
make-up bag	en **toilettaske**	ehn toaee**layt**aasker
make-up remover pads	nogle **vatrondeller**	nōāler vahtroan**day**lerr
mascara	en **mascara**	ehn mah**sk**arah
nail brush	en **neglebørste**	ehn **nigh**lerburster
nail clippers	en **negleklipper**	ehn **nigh**lerkleeberr
nail file	en **neglefil i stål**	ehn **nigh**lerfēēl ee stawl
nail polish	en **neglelak**	ehn **nigh**lerlahk
nail polish remover	en **neglelakfjerner**	ehn **nigh**lerlahkfyærnerr
nail scissors	en **neglesaks**	ehn **nigh**lersahks
nail strengthener	en **negleforstærker**	ehn **nigh**lerforstærkerr
paper handkerchiefs	**papirlommetørklæder**	pahp**ēēr**loamerturklaidherr

perfume	en parfume	ehn pahr**fewm**er
powder puff	en pudderkvast	ehn **poodherr**kvahst
rouge	noget rouge	n**oa**ert "rouge"
safety pins	nogle sikkerheds-nåle	n**oa**ler **siggerr**hehdhsnaw-ler
shampoo	noget shampoo	n**oa**ert **shahm**poa
shaving brush	en barberkost	ehn bahr**bayr**koast
shaving cream	en barbercreme	ehn bahr**bayr**kraym
shaving soap	et stykke barber-sæbe	eht **stewgg**er bahr**bayr**-saiber
soap	et stykke sæbe	eht **stewgg**er **saiber**
sun-tan cream/oil	noget solcreme/sololie	n**oa**ert **soal**kraym/**soal**oal-yer
talcum powder	noget talkum	n**oa**ert **tahl**koom
tissues	nogle ansigts-servietter	n**oa**ler **ahn**seegtssayrv**ee**-ehderr
toilet paper	noget toiletpapir	n**oa**ert toaee**layt**pahp**ee**r
toilet water	noget toiletvand	n**oa**ert toaee**layt**vahn
toothbrush	en tandbørste	ehn **tahn**burrster
toothpaste	en tube tandpasta	ehn t**oo**ber **tahn**pahstah
towel	et håndklæde	eht **hawn**klaidher
tweezers	en pincet	ehn peen**sayt**
washcloth	en vaskeklud	ehn **vahs**kerkl**oo**dh

For your hair

bobby pins	nogle hårklemmer	n**oa**ler **hawr**klaymerr
comb	en kam	ehn kahm
dye	noget farve	n**oa**ert **fahr**ver
grips	nogle hårklemmer	n**oa**ler **hawr**klaymerr
hair brush	en hårbørste	ehn **hawr**burrster
hair net	et hårnet	eht **hawr**nayt
hair oil	noget hårolie	n**oa**ert **hawr**oalyer
hair spray	noget hårlak	n**oa**ert **hawr**lahk
rollers	nogle ruller	n**oa**ler **rooll**err
setting lotion	noget setting-lotion	n**oa**ert "setting-lotion"

For the baby

baby cream	noget baby-creme	n**oa**ert "baby"-kraym
baby food	noget baby-mad	n**oa**ert "baby"-mahdh
baby powder	noget baby-pudder	n**oa**ert "baby"-**poodh**err
bib	en hagesmæk	ehn **haa**ersmehk
dummy (pacifier)	en narresut	ehn **nahr**ers**oo**t
nappies (diapers)	nogle bleer	n**oa**ler **blay**err
nappy pins	nogle blenåle	n**oa**ler **blay**nawler
plastic pants	nogle gummibukser	n**oa**ler **goom**meebookserr

SHOPPING GUIDE

Clothing

If you want to buy something specific, prepare yourself in advance. Look at the list of clothing on page 117. Get some idea of the colour, material and size you want. They're all listed on the next few pages.

General

I'd like...	**Jeg vil gerne have...**	yigh veel **geh**rner hæ
I want...for a 10-year-old boy.	**Jeg ønsker...til en 10-års dreng.**	yigh **urn**skerr...til ehn 10-awrss drayng
I want something like this.	**Jeg vil gerne have noget i denne stil.**	yigh veel **geh**rner hæ n**ōā**ert ee **deh**ner st**ēē**l
How much is that per metre?	**Hvad koster det pr. meter?**	vahdh **koa**sterr day pehr **maȳ**dherr

1 centimetre	= 2/5 in.	1 inch	= 2.54 cm.
1 metre	= 3 ft. 3⅜ in.	1 foot	= 30.5 cm.
10 metres	= 32 ft. 9¾ in.	1 yard	= 0.91 m.

Colour

I want something in...	**Jeg ønsker noget i...**	yigh **urn**skerr n**ōā**ert ee
I want a darker shade.	**Jeg ønsker en mørkere nuance.**	yigh **urn**skerr ehn **murr**kerer newahnsser
I want something to match this.	**Jeg ønsker noget, der passer til dette.**	yigh **urn**skerr n**ōā**ert dayr **pah**sserr til **deh**der
I don't like the colour.	**Jeg kan ikke lide farven.**	yigh kehn **ig**ger l**ēē**dher **fah**rvern

ensfarvet	**stribet**	**prikket**	**ternet**	**mønstret**
ehnsfahrvert	**stree**bert	**prig**gert	**tayr**nert	**murn**strert

beige	**beige**	"beige"
black	**sort**	soart
blue	**blå**	blaw
brown	**brun**	brōōn
cream	**cremefarvet**	kraymfahrvert
crimson	**højrød**	hoirurdh
emerald	**smaragdgrøn**	smaaraadhgrurn
fawn	**lysebrun**	lewsserbrōōn
gold	**guld**	gool
green	**grøn**	grurn
grey	**grå**	graw
mauve	**lilla**	leelaa
orange	**orange**	oaraansher
pink	**lyserød**	lewsserrurdh
purple	**violet**	vēēoalayt
red	**rød**	rurdh
scarlet	**skarlagensrød**	skahrlaaernsrurdh
silver	**sølv**	surl
tan	**gyldenbrun**	gewlernbrōōn
turquoise	**turkis**	tewrkēēss
white	**hvid**	veedh
yellow	**gul**	gōōl

Material

Do you have anything in…?	**Har De noget i…?**	haar dee nōāert ee
I want a cotton blouse.	**Jeg ønsker en bomuldsbluse.**	yigh urnsker ehn boamoolsblōōsser
Is it…?	**Er det…?**	ayr day
a permanent crease	**en varig pressefold**	ehn vaaree praysserfoal
hand made	**håndårbejde**	hawnahrbighder
imported	**importeret**	impoartāyrert
made here	**lavet her**	laavert hayr
synthetic	**syntetisk**	sewntāydeesk
tapered	**taljeret (med indsnit)**	taalyehrert (maydh insneet)
wash and wear	**til dryp-vask**	til drewp-vahsk
wrinkle free	**krølfrit**	krurlfreet
I want something…	**Jeg ønsker noget…**	yigh urnskerr nōāert
lighter/heavier	**lettere/sværere**	lehderrer/sværerrer
Do you have any better quality?	**Har De en bedre kvalitet?**	haar dee ehn behdhrer kvaaleetāyt

What's it made of?	**Hvad er det lavet af?**	vahdh ayr day laavert ah

It may be made of...

cambric	**batist**	bah**teest**
camel hair	**kamelhår**	kahmehlhawr
chiffon	**silkemusselin**	seelkermoosser**leen**
corduroy	**riflet fløjl**	reeflert floil
cotton	**bomuld**	boamool
denim	**deninstof**	dehne̱enstof
felt	**filt**	feelt
flannel	**flonel**	floanayl
gabardine	**gabardine**	gahbahrde̱ener
lace	**knipling**	knipleeng
leather	**læder**	laidherr
linen	**lærred**	læ̱rerdh
nylon	**nylon**	"nylon"
pique	**piké**	peekay
poplin	**poplin**	poaplin
rayon	**rayon**	rahyon
satin	**satin**	sahtin
seersucker	**bæk-og-bølge**	behk-oa-burlyer
serge	**uldserges**	oolsayrerss
silk	**silke**	seelker
suede	**ruskind**	rooskeen
taffeta	**taft**	tahft
towelling	**frotté**	froatay
tulle	**tyl**	tewl
tweed	**tweed**	"tweed"
velvet	**glat fløjl**	ghlaht floil
velveteen	**bomuldsfløjl**	boamoolsfloil
velour	**fløjl (uld)**	floil (ool)
wool	**uld**	ool
worsted	**kamgarn**	kahmgahrn

Size

My size is 38.	**Jeg bruger størrelse 38.**	yigh brooerr stu̱rrerlsser 38
Could you measure me?	**Vil De tage mine mål?**	veel dee tæ me̱ener mawl
I don't know the Danish sizes.	**Jeg kender ikke de danske størrelser.**	yigh kehnerr igger dee dahnsker stu̱rrerlsserr

In that case, look at the charts on the next page.

This is your size

Ladies

Dresses/Suits					
American	10	12	14	16	18	20
British	32	34	36	38	40	42
Continental	38	40	42	44	46	48

Stockings							Shoes			
American British	8	8½	9	9½	10	10½	6	7	8	9
							4½	5½	6½	7½
Continental	0	1	2	3	4	5	37	38	40	41

Gentlemen

Suits/Overcoats							Shirts			
American British	36	38	40	42	44	46	15	16	17	18
Continental	46	48	50	52	54	56	38	41	43	45

Shoes									
American British	5	6	7	8	8½	9	9½	10	11
Continental	38	39	41	42	43	43	44	44	45

In Europe sizes vary somewhat from country to country, so the above must be taken as an approximate guide.

A good fit?

Can I try it on?	Må jeg prøve den?	maw yigh **prur°°**er dehn
Where's the fitting room?	Hvor er prøve-rummet?	vōār ayr **prur°°**erroommert
Is there a mirror?	Er der et spejl?	ayr dayr eht spighl
Does it fit?	Passer den?	**pahss**err dehn

FOR NUMBERS, see page 175

SHOPPING GUIDE

It fits very well.	**Den sidder perfekt.**	dehn **seedherr** payr**faykt**
It doesn't fit.	**Den passer ikke.**	dehn **pahsserr** igger
It's too...	**Den er for...**	dehn ayr foar
short/long	**kort/lang**	koart/lahng
tight/loose	**snæver/vid**	snæverr/vee
How long will it take to alter?	**Hvor lang tid vil det tage at få den ændret?**	vōar lahng teedh veel day tæ aht faw dehn **ehndrert**

Shoes

I'd like a pair of...	**Jeg vil gerne have et par...**	yigh veel **gehr**ner hæ eht pahr
shoes/sandals	**sko/sandaler**	skoa/sahn**daa**lerr
boots/slippers	**støvler/hjemmesko**	stur°°lerr/**yaym**erskoa
These are too...	**De her er for...**	dee hayr ayr foar
narrow/wide	**smalle/brede**	**smah**ler/**bray**dher
large/small	**store/små**	**stoa**rer/smaw
They pinch my toes.	**De klemmer tæerne.**	dee **klay**merr **tæ**erner
Do you have a larger size?	**Har De et større nummer?**	haar dee eht **stür**rer **noom**merr
I want a smaller size.	**Jeg ønsker et mindre nummer.**	yigh **urns**kerr eht **min**drer **noom**merr
Do you have the same in...?	**Har De det samme par i...?**	haar dee day **sah**mer pahr ee
brown/beige	**brunt/beige**	brōōnt /''beige''
black/white	**sort/hvidt**	soart/veed
I'd like some shoe polish/shoe laces.	**Jeg vil gerne have noget skocreme/ et par snørebånd.**	yigh veel **gehr**ner hæ nōāert skoakraym/eht pahr snūrrerbawn

Shoes worn out? Here's the key to getting them repaired:

Can you repair these shoes?	**Kan De reparere disse sko?**	kehn dee raypah**ray**rer **dees**ser skoa
I want new soles and heels.	**Jeg ønsker forsåling og nye hæle.**	yigh **urns**kerr forsaw-leeng oa **nēw**er hailer
When will they be ready?	**Hvornår er de færdige?**	vor**nawr** ayr dee **fær**dēēer
I'd like a shine.	**Jeg vil gerne have dem pudset.**	yigh veel **gehr**ner hæ dehm **poos**sert

Clothes and accessories

I'd like a/an/some...	Jeg vil gerne have...	yigh veel **gehr**ner hæ
anorak	en anorak	ehn ahnoarahk
bathing cap	en badehætte	ehn baadherhehder
bathing suit	en badedragt	ehn baadherdrahgt
bath robe	en badekåbe	ehn baadherkawber
blouse	en bluse	ehn blōōsser
bra	en b.h.	ehn bay-haw
briefs	et par herreunder-benklæder	eht pahr **hehr**erooner-behnklaidherr
cap	en kasket	ehn **kaas**kayt
cardigan	en cardigan	ehn **kahr**digahn
coat	frakke	ehn **frah**gger
costume	en dragt	ehn drahgt
dress	en kjole	ehn kyoaler
dressing gown	en slåbrok	ehn slawbroak
evening dress (ladies)	en aftenkjole	ehn **ahf**ternkyoaler
fur coat	en pelsfrakke	ehn **payls**frahgger
galoshes	et par galocher	eht pahr gaaloasherr
garter belt	en strømpeholder	ehn strurmperhoalerr
girdle	en hofteholder	ehn **hoaf**terhoalerr
gloves	et par handsker	et pahr **hahns**kerr
handkerchief	et lommetørklæde	eht **loam**erturrklaidher
hat	en hat	ehn haht
jacket	en jakke	ehn **jah**gger
jeans	et par cowboy-bukser	eht pahr koboibookserr
jersey	un ulden trøje	ehn oolern troier
jumper (Br.)	en jumper	ehn "jumper"
jumper (Am.)	et forklæde	eht **foar**klaidher
lingerie	noget dameunder-tøj	nōært **daam**eroonertoi
nightdress	en natkjole	ehn **naht**kyoaler
overalls	et par overalls	eht pahr o°°erawl
overcoat	en overfrakke	ehn o°°erfrahgger
panties (ladies/children)	et par underben-klæder (dame-/børne-)	eht pahr oonerbehnklai-dherr (**daam**er-/**burr**ner-)
pants suit	en buksedragt	ehn bookserdrahgt
panty-girdle	et par panties	eht pahr "panties"
panty hose	et par strømpe-bukser	eht pahr strurmperbookserr
pullover	en pullover	ehn "pullover"
pyjamas	en pyjamas	ehn pewyaamaass
raincoat	en regnfrakke	ehn **righn**frahgger
rubber boots	et par gummistøvler	eht pahr goommeestur°°lerr

sandals	**et par sandaler**	eht pahr sahndaalerr
scarf	**et tørklæde**	eht turrklaidherr
shirt	**en skjorte**	ehn **skyoarter**
shoes	**et par sko**	eht pahr skoa
shorts	**et par shorts**	eht pahr shorts
skirt	**en nederdel**	ehn **nehdherdehl**
slippers	**et par hjemmesko**	eht pahr **yaymerskoa**
sneakers	**et par gymnastik-sko**	eht pahr gewmnah**steek**-skoa
socks	**et par sokker**	eht pahr **soaggerr**
stockings	**et par strømper**	eht pahr **strurmperr**
suit (men's)	**en habit**	ehn haa**beet**
suit (ladies')	**en spadseredragt**	ehn spahs**āy**rerdrahgt
suspender belt	**en strømpeholder**	ehn **strurmperhoalerr**
sweater	**en sweater**	ehn "sweater"
sweatshirt	**en træningsbluse**	ehn traineengsbl**ōō**sser
swimsuit	**en badedragt**	ehn **baadherdrahgt**
T-shirt	**en T-shirt**	ehn "T-shirt"
tennis shoes	**et par tennissko**	eht pahr **tehnisskoa**
tie	**et slips**	eht sleeps
tights	**et par strømpe-bukser**	eht pahr **strurmperbookser**
towel	**et håndklæde**	eht **hawnklaidher**
trousers	**et par bukser**	eht pahr **bookser**
twinset	**et cardigansæt**	eht **kahr**digahnseht
umbrella	**en paraply**	ehn pahrah**plew**
underpants (men's)	**et par herreunder-benklæder**	eht pahr **hehr**eroonerr-behnklaidherr
undershirt	**en undertrøje**	ehn **oonerrtroier**
vest (Am.)	**en vest**	ehn vayst
vest (Br.)	**en undertrøje**	ehn **oonerrtroier**
waistcoat	**en vest**	ehn vayst

belt	**et bælte**	eht **behlter**
buckle	**et spænde**	eht **spainer**
button	**en knap**	ehn knahp
collar	**en krave**	ehn **kraaver**
cuffs	**et par manchetter**	eht pahr **mahnshayderr**
elastic	**noget elastik**	n**ō**ãert ehlah**steek**
hem	**en søm**	ehn surm
lapel	**en revers**	ehn rayv**āy**r
lining	**et for**	eht foar
pocket	**en lomme**	ehn **loamer**
ribbon	**et bånd**	eht bawn
sleeve	**et ærme**	eht **ærmer**
zip (zipper)	**en lynlås**	ehn **lewnlawss**

Electrical appliances and accessories—Records

The voltage is 220 AC, 50 cps. An adaptor may come in handy.

I want a plug for this.	**Jeg vil gerne have et stik til denne her.**	yigh veel **gehr**ner hæ eht steek til **deh**ner hayr
Do you have a battery for this…?	**Har De et batteri til denne…?**	haar dee eht bahder**ree** til **deh**ner
This is broken. Can you repair it?	**Den er i stykker. Kan De reparere den?**	dehn ayr ee **stew**ggerr. kehn dee raypah**ray**rer dehn
When will it be ready?	**Hvornår er den færdig?**	vor**nawr** ayr dehn **fær**dee
I'd like a/an/some…	**Jeg vil gerne have…**	yigh veel **gehr**ner hæ
adaptor	**et mellemstik**	eht **may**lermsteek
amplifier	**en forstærker**	ehn for**stær**kerr
battery	**et batteri**	eht bahder**ree**
blender	**en blænder**	ehn **bleh**nder
clock	**et ur**	eht **ōōr**
food mixer	**en røremaskine**	ehn **rūr**rermaask**ēē**ner
hair dryer	**en hårtørrer**	ehn **hawr**turrerr
iron	**et strygejern**	eht **strew**eryærn
travelling-iron	**et rejsestrygejern**	eht **righss**erstreweryærn
kettle	**en kedel**	ehn **keh**dherl
percolator	**en kaffemaskine**	ehn **kah**fermaask**ēē**ner
plug	**et stik**	eht steek
radio	**en radio**	ehn **rah**dyoa
car radio	**en bilradio**	ehn **bēē**lrahdyoa
portable radio	**en transistor-radio**	ehn trahn**sees**torahdyoa
razor	**en barbermaskine**	ehn bahr**bāy**rmaask**ēē**ner
record player	**en pladespiller**	ehn **plaad**herspeelerr
portable record player	**en rejse-grammofon**	ehn **righss**ergrahmoaf**ōā**n
tape recorder	**en båndoptager**	ehn **bawn**optaaer
cassette tape recorder	**en kassette-båndoptager**	ehn kaas**say**der-**bawn**optaaer
portable tape recorder	**en transportabel båndoptager**	ehn trahnspoart**aaberl** **bawn**optaaer
television	**et fjernsyn**	eht **fyær**nsewn
portable television	**et transportabelt fjernsyn**	eht trahnspoart**aaberlt** **fyær**nsewn
toaster	**en brødrister**	ehn **brur**dhreesterr
transformer	**en transformator**	ehn transfoarm**aa**toar

Record shop

Do you have any records by...?	**Har De nogle plader med...?**	haar dee nōāler plaadherr maydh
Do you have...'s latest album?	**Har De...s sidste pladealbum?**	haar dee ...s seester plaadherahlboom
Can I listen to this record?	**Må jeg høre denne plade?**	maw yigh hūrrer dehner plaadher
I'd like a cassette/ cartridge.	**Jeg vil gerne have en kassette/kassette med 8 spor.**	yigh veel gehrner hæ ehn kaassāyder/kaassāyder maydh 8 spōar
I want a new stylus.	**Jeg vil gerne have en ny stift.**	yigh veel gehrner hæ en new steeft

33/45 rpm mono/stereo	**33/45 omdrejninger mono/stereo**	33/45 oamdrighneengerr moanoa/stehryoa

chamber music	**kammermusik**	kahmerrmoosseek
classical music	**klassisk musik**	klahseessk mooseek
folk music	**folkemusik**	foalkermoosseek
instrumental music	**instrumentalmusik**	instroomayntaal moosseek
jazz	**jazz**	"jazz"
light music	**let musik**	leht moosseek
orchestral music	**orkestermusik**	oarkaysterrmoosseek
pop music	**popmusik**	popmoosseek

Hairdressing—Barber's

I don't speak much Danish.	**Jeg taler ikke meget dansk.**	yigh **tailerr igger** **mighert** dahnsk
I'm in a hurry.	**Jeg har travlt.**	yigh haar trowlt
I want a haircut, please.	**Jeg vil gerne klippes.**	yigh veel **gehrner** **kleeberss**
I'd like a shave.	**Jeg vil gerne barberes.**	yigh veel **gehrner** bahr**bāȳr**erss
Don't cut it too short.	**Det skal ikke klippes for kort.**	day skahl **igger kleeberss** foar koart
Scissors only, please.	**Kun med saks, tak.**	koon maydh sahks tæk
A razor cut, please.	**Skåret med barber-blad.**	skawrert maydh bahr**bāȳr**-blaadh
Don't use the clippers.	**Brug ikke klippe-maskinen.**	broo **igger kleeber**-maask**ēē**nern
Just a trim, please.	**Bare en studsning.**	baarer ehn **stooss**neeng
That's enough off.	**Nu er det kort nok.**	noo ayr day koart noak
A little more off the...	**Lidt mere af...**	lit **māȳr**er ah
back	**bagtil**	baatil
neck	**i nakken**	ee **nahggern**
sides	**i siderne**	ee s**ēē**dherner
top	**ovenpå hovedet**	o°°ernpaw ho°°erdhert
Please don't use any oil/cream.	**Brug venligst ingen brillantine/creme.**	broo **vehnleest ingern** breelahnt**ēē**ner/kraym
Would you please trim my...?	**Vær venlig at studse...**	vær **vehnlee** aht **stoosser**
beard	**mit skæg**	meet skehg
moustache	**mit overskæg**	meet o°°erskehg
sideboards (side-burns)	**mine bakkenbarter**	m**ēē**ner bahg**gern**bahrterr
Thank you. That's fine.	**Tak. Det er fint.**	tæk. day ayr feent
How much do I owe you?	**Hvor meget bliver det?**	v**ōā**r **mighert** bl**ēē**err day

FOR TIPPING, see page 1

Ladies' hairdresser's—Beauty salon

| Can I make an appointment for sometime on Thursday? | **Kan jeg få en tid på torsdag?** | kehn yigh faw ehn teedh paw toarsdai |
| I'd like it cut and shaped. | **Jeg vil gerne have det klippet og vandonduleret.** | yigh veel gehrner hæ day kleebert oa vahnoandoolehrert |

with a fringe (bangs)	**med pandehår**	maydh paanerhawr
page-boy style	**pagehår**	paasherhawr
a razor cut	**skåret med barberblad**	skawrert maydh bahrbāȳrblaadh
a re-style	**en ny frisure**	ehn new freessēwrer
with ringlets	**med lokker**	maydh loaggerr
with waves	**med bølger**	maydh burlyerr
in a bun	**i en knude**	ee ehn knoodher

I want a...	**Jeg ønsker...**	yigh urnskerr
bleach	**en afblegning**	ehn owblighneeng
colour rinse	**en skylning**	ehn skewlneeng
dye	**en farvning**	ehn fahrvneeng
permanent wave	**en permanent**	ehn payrmaanaynt
shampoo and set	**en vask og vandondulation**	ehn vahsk oa vahn-oandoolasyoan
tint	**en toning**	ehn toaneeng
touch up	**en opfriskning af farven**	opfreeskneeng ah fahrvern

I want...	**Jeg ønsker...**	yigh urnskerr
the same colour	**den samme farve**	dehn sahmer fahrver
a darker colour	**en mørkere tone**	ehn murrkerrer toaner
a lighter colour	**en lysere farve**	ehn lewsserrer fahrver
auburn/blond/brunette	**kastaniebrun/blond/brunette**	kahstaanyerbrōōn/bloan/broonāȳder

Do you have a colour chart?	**Har De et farvekort?**	haar dee eht fahrverkoart
I don't want any hairspray.	**Jeg ønsker ikke hårlak.**	yigh urnskerr igger hawrlahk
I want a...	**Jeg ønsker...**	yigh urnskerr
manicure/pedicure	**en manicure/pedicure**	ehn maaneekēwrer/pehdee-kēwrer
face-pack	**en ansigtsmaske**	ehn ahnseegtsmahsker

FOR TIPPING, see page 1

Jeweller's—Watchmaker's

Danish artisans work in gold and platinum, silver, steel, pewter and copper. You'll find Danish craftsmanship expressed in modern as well as traditional designs for jewellery and other objects.

Can you repair this watch?	**Kan De reparere dette ur?**	kehn dee raypahr**ay**rer dehder **oo**r
The… is broken.	**… er gået i stykker.**	ayr gawert ee **stewg**gerr
glass/spring strap/winder	**glasset/fjederen remmen/optrækket**	**glahs**sert/**fyehd**herrern raymern/op**træg**gert
When will it be ready?	**Hvornår er det færdigt?**	vornawr ayr day **fær**deet
Could I please see that?	**Må jeg se det dér?**	maw yigh s**ay** day dayr
I'm just looking around.	**Jeg kigger mig blot omkring.**	yigh **kigg**err migh bloat oam**kring**
I'd like a cheap watch.	**Jeg vil gerne have et billigt ur.**	yigh veel **geh**rner hæ eht **beeleet oo**r
I want a small gift.	**Jeg ønsker at købe en lille gave.**	yigh **urn**skerr aht k**ur**ber ehn **leel**er gaaver
I don't want anything too expensive.	**Jeg vil ikke have noget, der er for dyrt.**	yigh veel **igg**er hæ n**oa**ert dayr ayr foar dewrt
I want something…	**Jeg ønsker noget…**	yigh **urn**skerr n**oa**ert
better	**bedre**	**behd**hrer
cheaper	**billigere**	**beel**ēēerrer
simpler	**mere enkelt**	**may**rer **ayn**kerlt
Do you have anything in gold?	**Har De noget i guld?**	haar dee n**oa**ert ee gool
How many carats is this?	**Hvor mange karat er dette?**	v**oa**r **mahn**ger kahraht ayr dehder
Is this real silver?	**Er det ægte sølv?**	ayr day **ehg**ter surl
Can you engrave my initials on it?	**Kan jeg få mine initialer indgraveret på den?**	kehn yigh faw **mee**ner eeneet**ēē**ailerr ingrah**vay**rert paw dehn

SHOPPING GUIDE

When you go to a jeweller's, you've probably got some idea of what you want beforehand. Using the following lists, find out what the article is called and what it's made of.

What is it?

I'd like a/an/some...	Jeg vil gerne have...	yigh veel **gehrner** hæ
beads	nogle (uægte) perler	nō**ā**ler (ōōehgter) pa̅yrlerr
bracelet	et armbånd	eht **ahrm**bawn
brooch	en broche	ehn **broash**er
chain	en kæde	ehn **kaid**her
charm	et vedhæng	eht va̅**y**dhhehng
cigarette case	et cigaretetui	eht **siggahr**ay**deht**ooē̄
cigarette lighter	en lighter	ehn **lighter**
clock	et ur	eht ōōr
alarm clock	et vækkeur	eht **vehg**gerōōr
travelling clock	et rejseur	eht **righs**serōōr
cross	et kors	eht koarss
cuff-links	nogle manchet-knapper	nō**ā**ler mahn**shayt**knahberr
cutlery	noget spisebestik	nō**ā**ert spē**ē**sserbersteek
earrings	et par ørenringe	eht pahr **ūr**rernreenger
jewel box	et smykkeskrin	eht **smewg**gerskrē**ē**n
manicure set	et manicuresæt	eht **maaneek**ē̄w**r**ersayt
mechanical pencil	en skrueblyant	ehn skrōō**er**blewahnt
necklace	en halskæde	ehn **hahls**kaidher
pendant	et halssmykke	eht **haals**smewgger
pin	en nål	ehn nawl
powder compact	en pudderdåse	ehn **poodh**erdawsser
propelling pencil	en skrueblyant	ehn skrōō**er**blewahnt
ring	en ring	ehn reeng
engagement ring	forlovelsesring	foarlo**°°erls**sersreeng
signet ring	signetring	see**neht**reeng
wedding ring	vielsesring	vē**ē**erlss**er**sreeng
silverware	noget sølvtøj	nō**ā**ert **surl**toi
strap	en rem	ehn raym
tie clip	en slipseklemme	ehn **sleep**serklaymer
tie pin	en slipsenål	ehn **sleep**sernawl
watch	et ur	eht ōōr
calendar watch	et ur med dato	eht ōōr maydh **daat**oa
pocket watch	et lommeur	eht **loam**erōōr
wristwatch	et armbåndsur	eht **ahrm**bawnsōōr
shock resistant	stødsikkert	**sturdh**seeggert

waterproof	**vandtæt**	**vahn**teht
with a seconds hand	**med sekundviser**	maydh sehkoonvēēsserr
watch band	**en urrem**	ehn ōōrraym
expansion band	**en fixoflex-rem**	ehn feeksoa**flayks**-raym
leather band	**en læderrem**	ehn **laidh**erraym

What's it made of?

alabaster	**alabast**	aalaa**bahst**
amber	**rav**	row
amethyst	**ametyst**	ahmer**tewst**
brass	**messing**	**mays**seeng
bronze	**bronze**	**broan**sser
chromium	**krom**	kroam
copper	**kobber**	**koa**err
coral	**koral**	**koa**rahl
crystal	**krystal**	krew**stahl**
cut glass	**slebet glas**	**sleh**bert glahss
diamond	**diamant**	**dee**aa**mahnt**
ebony	**ibenholt**	**ēē**bernhoalt
emerald	**smaragd**	smaa**rahd**
enamel	**emalje**	eh**mal**yer
glass	**glas**	glahss
gold	**guld**	gool
gold plate	**gulddoublé**	**gool**dooblāy
ivory	**elfenben**	**ayl**fernbāyn
jade	**jade**	**yaad**her
marble	**marmor**	**mahr**moar
onyx	**onyks**	**oa**newks
pearl	**perle**	**pāy**rler
pewter	**tin**	tin
platinum	**platin**	plaa**tēēn**
ruby	**rubin**	roo**bēēn**
sapphire	**safir**	saa**fēēr**
silver	**sølv**	surl
silver plate	**pletsølv**	**playt**surl
stainless steel	**rustfrit stål**	**roost**freet stawl
sterling silver	**sterling sølv**	**stāy**rleeng surl
topaz	**topas**	toa**paass**
turquoise	**turkis**	tewr**kēēss**

SHOPPING GUIDE

Laundry—Dry-cleaning

If your hotel doesn't have its own laundry or dry-cleaning service, ask the desk clerk:

Where's the nearest laundry/dry-cleaner's?	**Hvor er det nærmeste vaskeri/ renseri?**	vōar ayr day **nǣr**merster vahsker**ree**/rayns**serree**
I want these clothes...	**Jeg vil gerne have dette tøj...**	yigh veel **gehr**ner hæ **deh**der toi
cleaned	**renset**	**rayns**sert
ironed	**strøget**	**stroi**ert
pressed	**presset**	**prays**sert
washed	**vasket**	**vahs**kert
When will it be ready?	**Hvornår er det færdigt?**	vornawr ayr day **fær**deet
I need it...	**Jeg skal bruge det...**	yigh skahl **brōō**er day
today	**i dag**	ee dai
tonight	**i aften**	ee **ahf**tern
tomorrow	**i morgen**	ee **mōā**ern
before Friday	**før fredag**	fūrr **fray**dai
I want it as soon as possible.	**Jeg vil gerne have det snarest muligt.**	yigh veel **gehr**ner hæ day **snah**rerst **mōō**leet
Can you...this?	**Kan De...det her?**	kehn dee...day hayr
mend	**reparere**	raypah**rāy**rer
patch	**lappe**	**lah**ber
stitch	**sy**	sew
Can you sew on this button?	**Vil De sy denne knap i?**	veel de sew **deh**ner knahp ee
Can you get this stain out?	**Kan De fjerne denne plet?**	kehn dee fyǣrner **deh**ner playt
Can this be invisibly mended?	**Kan dette kunststoppes?**	kehn **deh**der **koonst**stoaberss
This isn't mine.	**Det her er ikke mit.**	day hayr ayr **igger** meet
There's one piece missing.	**Der mangler noget.**	dayr **mahng**lerr **nōā**ert
There's a hole in this.	**Der er et hul i dette.**	dayr ayr eht hool ee **deh**der
Is my laundry ready?	**Er mit vasketøj færdigt?**	ayr meet **vahs**kertoi **fær**deet

Photography—Cameras

I want an inexpensive camera.	**Jeg vil gerne have et billigt kamera.**	yigh veel **gehr**ner hæ eht **beel**eet **kaam**errah
Show me the one in the window.	**Vil De vise mig det, der er i vinduet?**	veel dee **vōōss**er migh day dayr ayr ee **veend**ōōert

Film

Film sizes aren't always indicated the same way as in Great Britain and the United States. The best thing to do when in difficulty is to show the shop assistant the kind of film you want, or point to it in the box below. You'll also find the list of translations useful.

110 = 13 × 17	**127** = 4 × 4
120 = 6 × 6	**135** = 24 × 36
126 = 6 × 6	**620** = 6 × 6

I'd like a...	**Jeg vil gerne have...**	yigh veel **gehr**ner hæ
film for this camera	**en film til dette apparat**	ehn feelm til **dehd**er ahbahr**aat**
colour film	**en farvefilm**	ehn **fahr**verfeelm
black and white film	**en sort/hvid film**	ehn soart/veedh feelm
Polaroid film	**en Polaroid film**	ehn poalahro**eedh** feelm
cartridge	**en film i kassette**	ehn feelm ee kaass**ay**der
20/36 exposures	**20/36 optagelser**	20/36 opt**aaerls**serr
this ASA/DIN number	**dette ASA-/DIN-nummer**	**dehd**er **aiss**ah-/**dēēn**-**noomm**err
fast film	**en hurtig film**	ehn **hoor**tee feelm
fine grain	**en finkornet film**	ehn **fēēn**koarnert feelm
colour negatives	**en film til farve-papirbilleder**	ehn feelm til **fahr**ver-pahp**ēēr**beelerdherr
colour reversal	**en film til farve-diapositiver**	ehn feelm til **fahr**ver-d**ēē**aapoasseet**ēē**verr
artificial light type (indoor)	**til indendørs optagelser**	til **inn**erndurrss opt**aaerls**serr
daylight type (outdoor)	**til udendørs optagelser**	till **ōōd**herndurrss opt**aaerls**serr
8-mm-film super 8	**8-mm film super 8**	8-milli**mayd**herr feelm **sōō**per 8
16-mm film	**16-mm film**	16-milli**mayd**herr feelm

FOR NUMBERS, see page 175

Processing

Does the price include processing?	**Er fremkaldelsen medregnet i prisen?**	ayr **fraymkahlerlssern maydhrighnert** ee **prēēssern**
Will you develop and print this?	**Vil De fremkalde og lave aftryk af dette?**	veel dee **fraymkahler** oa **laaver owtrewk** ah **dehder**
I want...prints of each negative.	**Jeg ønsker...aftryk af hvert negativ.**	yigh **urnskerr...owtrewk** ah vayrt **nehgahtēēv**
with a glossy finish	**med højglans**	maydh **hoiglahnss**
with a mat finish	**med mat overflade**	maydh maht o°°erflaadher
this size	**denne størrelse**	dehner **stūrrelsser**
this contact paper	**dette kontaktpapir**	dehder koan**tahkt**pahpēēr
Will you please enlarge this?	**Vil De forstørre dette?**	veel dee for**stūrr**er dehder
When will it be ready?	**Hvornår er det færdigt?**	vornawr ayr day **færdeet**

Accessories

I want a/an/some...	**Jeg vil gerne have...**	yigh veel **gehr**ner hæ
cable release	**en trådudløser**	ehn **trawdhōōdhlūrsserr**
camera case	**et kameraetui**	eht **kaam**errahehtooēē
electronic flash	**en elektron-flash**	ehn ehlayk**trōān**-flash
exposure meter	**en belysningsmåler**	ehn beh**lews**neengsmawlerr
filter	**et filter**	eht **feel**terr
polarizing	**polariserende**	poalahrees**ay**rrerner
red	**rødt**	rurt
ultra-violet	**ultra-violet**	ooltrah-vēēoalayt
yellow	**gult**	gōōlt
flash bulbs	**nogle blitzpærer**	nōāler **bleets**pærerr
flash cubes	**nogle blitz-terninger**	nōāler **bleets**-tayrneenger
lens	**et objektiv**	eht oab**yayktēēv**
telephoto	**et teleobjektiv**	eht **tay**leroabyayktēēv
wide-angle	**et vidvinkel-objektiv**	eht **vēēdh**veenkerl-oabyayktēēv
zoom	**et zoom-objektiv**	eht sōōm-oabyayktēēv
lens cap	**en objektivhætte**	ehn oab**yayktēē**vhehder
lens cleaners	**renseklude til objektivet**	**rayns**serklōōdher til oab**yayktēē**vert
lens hood	**en objektivbeskytter**	ehn oab**yayktēē**v-beh**skewd**er
tripod	**et stativ**	eht stah**tēēv**

Broken

This camera doesn't work. Can you repair it?	**Dette kamera virker ikke. Kan De reparere det?**	dehder kaamerrah veerker igger. kehn dee raypah-rāyrer day
The film is jammed.	**Filmen sidder fast.**	feelmern seedherr fahst
The knob won't turn.	**Knappen virker ikke.**	knahbern veerkerr igger
There's something wrong with the...	**Der er noget i vejen med...**	dayr ayr nōāert ee vighern maydh
automatic lens	**det automatiske objektiv**	day owtoamaateesker oabyayktēēv
exposure counter	**billedtælleren**	beeledhtehlerrern
diaphragm	**blænderen**	blainerrern
film feed	**filmfremføringen**	feelmframfūrreengern
flash contact	**blitzkontakten**	bleetskoantahktern
lens	**linsen**	leenssern
lightmeter	**belysningsmåleren**	behlewsneengsmawlerrern
rangefinder	**afstandsmåleren**	owstahnsmawlerrern
shutter	**lukkeren**	looggerrern

Shooting

People usually don't mind if you take their picture, but it's always best to ask first.

Do you mind if I take a few photographs?	**Har De noget imod at jeg tager et par billeder?**	haar dee nōāert eemoadh aht yigh taaer eht pahr beelerdherr
May I take a picture of you?	**Må jeg tage et billede af Dem?**	maw yigh tæ eht beelerdher ah dehm
Please stand over there.	**Vær venlig at stille Dem derovre.**	vær vehnlee aht steeler dehm dayro°°er
I'll send you a print.	**Jeg sender Dem en kopi.**	yigh saynerr dehm ehn koapee

And if you want to ask someone to take *your* picture:

Would you mind taking my/our picture? Press this button.	**Har De noget imod at tage et billede af mig/os? Tryk på denne knap.**	haar dee nōāert eemoadh aht tæ eht beelerdher ah migh/oss? trewk paw dehner knahp

Provisions

Here's a basic list of food and drink that you might want on a picnic or for the occasional meal at home:

I'd like a/an/some…	Jeg vil gerne have…	yigh veel **gehr**ner hæ
apples	nogle æbler	nōāler ehblerr
bananas	nogle bananer	nōāler bahnaanerr
biscuits (Br.)	nogle småkager	nōāler smawkaaerr
bread	noget brød	nōāert brurdh
butter	noget smør	nōāert smurr
cakes	nogle kager	nōāler kaaerr
candy	noget slik	nōāert slik
cheese	noget ost	nōāert oast
chocolate bar	en plade chokolade	ehn plaadher shoakoalaa-dher
coffee	noget kaffe	nōāert kahfer
cold cuts	noget pålæg	nōāert pawlehg
cookies	nogle småkager	nōāler smawkaaerr
crackers	nogle kiks	nōāler kiks
cream	noget fløde	nōāert flūrdher
crisps	nogle franske kartofler	nōāler frahnsker kahrtoafler
cucumbers	nogle agurker	nōāler ahgoorkerr
eggs	nogle æg	nōāler ehg
frankfurters	nogle bajerske pølser	nōāler bighersker purlsser
ham	noget skinke	nōāert skeenker
hamburgers	nogle hakkebøffer	nōāler hahggerburferr
ice-cream	noget is	nōāert ēēss
lemonade	noget limonade	nōāert leemoanaadher
lemons	nogle citroner	nōāler seetrōānerr
lettuce	noget (hoved) salat	nōāert (ho°°erdh) sahlaat
liver sausage	noget leverpølse	nōāert leh°°erpurlsser
milk	noget mælk	nōāert mehlk
mustard	noget sennep	nōāert sehnerp
noodles	nogle nudler	nōāler noodlerr
oranges	nogle appelsiner	nōāler ahberlsēēnerr
pepper	noget peber	nōāert peh°°er
pickles	noget pickles	nōāler peeklerss
potato chips (Am.)	nogle franske kartofler	nōāler frahnsker kahrtoaflerr
potatoes	nogle kartofler	nōāler kahrtoaflerr
rolls	nogle rundstykker	nōāler roonstewggerr
salad	noget salat	nōāert sahlaat
salami	noget spegepølse	nōāert spigherpurlsser

salt	**noget salt**	n<u>oa</u>ert sahlt
sausages	**nogle pølser**	n<u>oa</u>ler purlsser
sugar	**noget sukker**	n<u>oa</u>ert sooggerr
sweets	**noget slik**	n<u>oa</u>ert slik
tea	**noget te**	n<u>oa</u>ert teh
tomatoes	**nogle tomater**	n<u>oa</u>ler toamaaderr

And don't forget...

aluminium foil	**noget aluminiums-folie**	n<u>oa</u>ert ahloom<u>ee</u>n<u>ee</u>ooms-foalyer
bottle opener	**en flaskeåbner**	ehn flahskerawbnerr
corkscrew	**en proptrækker**	ehn proaptrehggerr
matches	**nogle tændstikker**	n<u>oa</u>ler tainstiggerr
paper napkins	**nogle papirs-servietter**	n<u>oa</u>ler pahp<u>ee</u>rssayr-v<u>ee</u>hderr
paper towelling	**en køkkenrulle**	ehn kurggernrooler
plastic bags	**nogle plasticposer**	n<u>oa</u>ler plahstikpoasserr
tin (can) opener	**en dåseåbner**	ehn dawsserawbnerr
wax paper	**noget pergament-papir**	n<u>oa</u>ert pehrgahm<u>ay</u>nt-pahp<u>ee</u>r

---

Weights and measures

1 kilogram or kilo (kg) = 1000 grams (g)

| 100 g = 3½ oz. | ½ kg = 1 lb. 1½ oz. |
| 200 g = 7 oz. | 1 kg = 2 lb. 3 oz. |

1 oz. = 28.35 g
1 lb. = 453.60 g

---

1 litre (l) = 0.88 imp. quarts = 1.06 U.S. quarts

| 1 imp. quart = 1.14 l | 1 U.S. quart = 0.95 l |
| 1 imp. gallon = 4.55 l | 1 U.S. gallon = 3.8 l |

---

box	**en æske**	ehn ehsker
can	**en dåse**	ehn dawsser
carton	**en karton**	ehn kahrtong
crate	**en trækasse**	ehn trehkahsser
jar	**en krukke**	ehn kroogger
packet	**en pakke**	ehn pahgger
tin	**en dåse**	ehn dawsser
tube	**en tube**	ehn t<u>oo</u>ber

PROVISIONS

Souvenirs

Danish handicrafts cover a wide range—textiles, ceramics, glassware and toys of notable good taste. Look for hand-made costumed dolls and long-fleeced woollen rugs. Hand-painted porcelain and modern-design household articles are famous. Other practical purchases include stylish furniture and antiques.

Here are some ideas for your shopping.

applied arts	kunsthåndværk	koonsthawnværk
aquavit	akvavit	ahkvahveet
amber	rav	row
antiques	antikviteter	ahnteekveetäyderr
candles	stearinlys	stayahrēēnlewss
ceramics	keramik	kehrahmēēk
chess set	et skakspil	eht skahkspeel
costumed doll	en dukke i folke-dragt	ehn doogger ee foalker-drahgt
embroidery	broderi	broaderree
furniture	møbler	mūrblerr
gadget	en sjov, lille ting	ehn sho°° leeler teeng
glassware	en glasting	ehn glahsteeng
hand-painted	håndmalet	hawnmaalert
modern	moderne	moadāyrnert
knitware	strikvarer	streekvaarerr
lamp	en lampe	ehn lahmper
poster	en plakat	ehn plahkaat
shag-rug	et rya-tæppe	eht rēwaa-taiber
woollen	uldent	oolernt
stamps	frimærker	freemærkerr
textiles	tekstilvarer	tayksteelvaarerr
hand-printed (textiles)	stoftryk	stoaftrewg
toys	legetøj	lighertoi

Tobacconist's

In Denmark the most popular brands have English-sounding names—*Prince, Queens, Kings, Cecil,* for example. All cigarettes are heavily taxed, making them quite expensive.

I'd like a/an/some...	Jeg vil gerne have ...	yigh veel **gehr**ner hæ
box of cigars	en æske cigarer	ehn **ehs**ker siggahrerr
cigar	en cigar	ehn siggahr
cigarette case	et cigaretetui	eht siggah**ray**tehtooee
cigarette holder	et cigaretrør	eht siggah**ray**trürr
cigarette lighter	en lighter	en "lighter"
flints	nogle sten (til en lighter)	**noa**ler stehn (til ehn "lighter"
lighter fluid	tændvæske til en lighter	**tain**vehsker til ehn "lighter"
lighter gas	gas til en lighter	gahss til ehn "lighter"
refill for a lighter	en refill til en lighter	ehn reh**feel** til ehn "lighter"
matches	tændstikker	**tain**stiggerr
packet of...	en pakke...	ehn **pah**gger
packet of cigarettes	en pakke cigaretter	ehn **pah**gger siggah**ray**derr
pipe	en pibe	ehn **pee**ber
pipe cleaners	nogle piberensere	**noa**ler **pee**berraynsserrer
pipe tobacco	noget pibetobak	**noa**ler **pee**bertoabahk
pipe tool	en pibekradser	ehn **pee**berkrahsserr
tobacco pouch	en tobakspung	ehn **toa**bahkspoong
wick	en væge	ehn **vai**er
Do you have any...?	Har De nogle...?	haar dee **noa**ler
American cigarettes	amerikanske cigaretter	ahmehreekaansker siggah**ray**derr
English cigarettes	engelske cigaretter	**ehn**gerlsker siggah**ray**derr
menthol cigarettes	mentolcigaretter	**mayn**toalsiggah**ray**derr
I'll take two packets.	Jeg tager to pakker.	yigh taar toa **pah**ggerr
I'd like a carton.	Jeg vil gerne have en karton.	yigh veel **gehr**ner hæ ehn **kah**rtong

filter-tipped	med filter	maydh **feel**terr
king-size	lange	**lahn**ger
without filter	uden filter	**ōō**dhern **feel**terr

Your money: banks—currency

You'll usually find someone who speaks English at any larger bank. Small currency-exchange offices (*vekselkontor*—**vayks**erlkoantoār) operate in most tourist centres. Signs usually announce CHANGE, written in English. The exchange rates don't vary much between banks and *vekselkontorer*. Remember to take your passport, since you'll probably need it as identification.

Travellers' cheques and credit cards are widely accepted in tourist-oriented shops, hotels, restaurants etc. However, if you're exploring the countryside off the beaten track you mustn't expect every little village store to be acquainted with them, or with foreign currency. The same applies to garages and service stations: large agency garages and service stations in the major towns will probably accept foreign currency, credit cards and travellers' cheques, but smaller establishments may not.

Opening hours

With minor variations from town to town, most banks are open from Monday to Friday from 9.30 a.m. to 3 p.m., with a late session on Thursday or Friday from 4 to 6 p.m. In Copenhagen, the exchange office at the city air terminal at the Central Railway Station stays open from 7 a.m. to 10 p.m. daily.

Monetary unit

Denmark, Norway and Sweden all use the same name for their currencies, but the value differs in each country. The Crown (*kronen*—**krōā**nern) is divided into 100 øre (**ūr**rer). The abbreviation is *kr.,* or sometimes *dkr.* to distinguish the Danish Crown from the Norwegian and Swedish.

There are coins of 5, 10 and 25 øre, 1, 5 and 10 kr., and notes of 20, 50, 100, 500 and 1000 kr.

Before going

Where's the nearest bank/currency-exchange office?	**Hvor er den nærmeste bank/det nærmeste vekselkontor?**	vōär ayr dehn **nä**rmerster bahnk/day **nä**rmerster **vayk**serlkoant**ōä**r
Where can I cash a traveller's cheque?	**Hvor kan jeg indløse en rejsecheck?**	vōär kehn yigh inl**ūr**sser ehn **righ**sserchayk
Where is the American Express?	**Hvor er American Express?**	vōär ayr "american express"

Inside

I want to change some dollars/pounds.	**Jeg vil gerne veksle nogle dollars/pund.**	yigh veel **geh**rner **vayk**sler **nōä**ler **doll**arss/poon
What's the exchange rate?	**Hvad er vekselkursen?**	vahdh ayr **vayk**serl**koor**ssern
What rate of comission do you charge?	**Hvor megen kommission beregner De?**	vōär **migh**ern koamee**sy**oan **ber**righnerr dee
Can you cash a personal cheque?	**Kan De indløse en personlig check?**	kehn dee inl**ūr**sser ehn payrs**ōä**nlee chayk
How long will it take to clear?	**Hvor lang tid tager det at kontrollere den?**	vōär lahng teedh taar day aht koantroal**ay**rer dehn
Can you wire my bank in...?	**Kan De telegrafere til min bank i...?**	kehn dee tehlergrah**fay**rer til m**ēē**n bahnk ee
I have...	**Jeg har...**	yigh haar
a letter of credit	**et kreditbrev**	eht krayd**eet**breh°°
an introduction from...	**en anbefaling fra...**	ehn **ahn**berfaaleeng fraa
a credit card	**et kreditkort**	eht krayd**eet**koart
I'm expecting some money from... Has it arrived yet?	**Jeg venter nogle penge fra... Er de kommet?**	yigh **vayn**terr **nōä**ler **payn**ger fraa... ayr deh **koa**mert
Please give me...in notes (bills) and some small change.	**Giv mig...i sedler og nogle småpenge.**	gee migh...ee **say**dlerr oa **nōä**ler **smaw**paynger
Give me...100-crown notes and the rest in small notes.	**Giv mig...hundredkronesedler og resten i mindre sedler.**	gee migh...**hoo**nrerdh-kr**ōä**ner**say**dlerr oa **ray**stern ee mindrer **say**dlerr
Could you please check that again?	**Vær venlig at kontrollere det igen.**	vær **vehn**lee aht koan-troal**ay**rer day eeg**gayn**

BANK

Depositing

I want to credit this to my account.	**Jeg ønsker at indsætte dette beløb på min konto.**	yigh **urn**skerr aht **inseh**der **deh**der beh**lurb** paw **mēēn koan**toa
I want to credit this to Mr...'s account.	**Jeg ønsker at kreditere dette til hr. ...s konto.**	yigh **urn**skerr aht kraydee**tāy**rer **deh**der til hehr ...s **koan**toa
Where should I sign?	**Hvor skal jeg kvittere?**	vōar skahl yigh kvee**tāy**rer

Currency converter

In a world of fluctuating exchange rates, we can offer no more than this do-it-yourself chart. You can get a card showing current exchange rates from banks, travel agents and tourist offices. Why not fill in this chart, too, for handy reference?

BANK

Crowns	£	$
10 øre		
50 øre		
1 krone		
10 kroner		
50 kroner		
100 kroner		
500 kroner		
1000 kroner		
5000 kroner		

FOR NUMBERS, see page 175

At the post office

In Denmark the post office is marked *Posthus* (**poast**hōōss).
Business hours are generally from 9 or 10 a.m. to 5 or
6 p.m. from Monday to Friday, and from 9 a.m. to noon on
Saturday. In the provinces, hours vary. Postboxes are
painted red.

Where's the (nearest) post office?	**Hvor er det (nærmeste) posthus?**	vōar ayr day (**næ**rmerster) poasthōōss
Can you tell me how to get to the post office?	**Kan De forklare mig vejen til posthuset?**	kehn dee forklahrer migh **vigh**ern til poasthōōssert
What time does the post office open/close?	**Hvornår åbner/lukker posthuset?**	vornawr awbnerr/**loo**ggerr poasthōōssert
What window do I go to for stamps?	**Ved hvilken luge kan jeg købe frimærker?**	vaydh vilkern lōōer kehn yigh **kū**ber freemærkerr
At which counter can I cash an international money order?	**Ved hvilken luge kan jeg indløse en international pengeanvisning?**	vaydh vilkern lōōer kehn yigh inlūrsser ehn internaasyoanaal paynger-ahnvēēsneeng
I want some stamps, please.	**Jeg vil gerne have nogle frimærker.**	vigh veel gehrner hæ nōaler freemærker
I want...60-øre stamps and...1-crown stamps.	**Jeg ønsker...60-øres frimærker og...til en krone.**	yigh urnsker...60-ūrrerss freemærkerr oa ...til ehn kroaner
What's the postage for a letter to England?	**Hvor meget skal der på et brev til England?**	vōar mighert skahl dayr paw eht brehᵒᵒ til ehnglahn
What's the postage for a postcard to the U.S.A.?	**Hvor meget skal der på et postkort til USA?**	vōar mighert skahl dayr paw eht **poast**-kōart til oo-ehss-ai
I want to send this parcel.	**Jeg ønsker at sende denne pakke.**	yigh urnskeʰr aht sayner dehner **pah**gger
Do I need to fill in a customs declaration?	**Skal jeg udfylde en toldformular?**	skahl yigh **ōō**dhfewler ehn **toal**foarmoolahr

Where's the mail-box?	**Hvor er postkassen?**	vōār ayr **poast**kahssern
I want to send this by...	**Jeg ønsker at sende dette...**	yigh **ur**nskerr aht **sayner dehd**er
airmail	**pr. luftpost**	pehr **looft**poast
express (special delivery)	**ekspres**	ehk**sprayss**
registered mail	**anbefalet**	ahnberfaalert
small parcel	**som brevpakke**	soam **breh**°°**pah**gger
surface mail	**med almindelig postbefordring**	maydh **ahl**meennerlee **poast**berfoardreeng
Where's the poste restante (general delivery)?	**Hvor er der poste restante?**	vōār ayr dayr **poast**er raystaanter
Is there any mail for me? My name is...	**Er der noget post til mig? Mit navn er...**	ayr dayr **nōā**ert poast til migh. meet nown ayr
Here's my passport.	**Her er mit pas.**	hayr ayr meet pahss

FRIMÆRKER	STAMPS
PAKKER	PARCELS
UDBETALING	MONEY ORDERS

Telegrams

Cables and telegrams are dispatched by the post office.

Where's the (nearest) telegraph office?	**Hvor er (det nærmeste) telegrafkontor?**	vōār ayr (day **næ**rmerster) tehler**grahf**koantōār
I want to send a telegram. May I please have a form?	**Jeg vil gerne sende et telegram. Må jeg bede øm en blanket?**	yigh veel **gehr**ner **sayner** eht tehler**grahm**. maw yigh **behd**her oam ehn blahn**kayt**
How much is it per word?	**Hvad koster det pr. ord?**	vahdh **koa**sterr day pehr oar
I'd like to reverse the charges.	**Modtageren betaler.**	**moadh**taaerrern bertaaler
I'd like to send a night letter.	**Jeg vil gerne sende et nattelegram.**	yigh veel **gehr**ner **sayner** eht **nahd**ertehlergrahm

Telephoning

You can dial directly to most places in Denmark as well as the rest of Europe. STD (area) codes are listed in regional telephone books. To make a local call from a coin box, insert two 25-øre coins first. Some telephone booths require the use of cards (a *Telet*), obtained from kiosks all over the town.

General

Where's the telephone?	**Hvor er telefonen?**	vōār ayr tehlerfōānern
Where's there a public telephone?	**Hvor er der en offentlig telefonboks?**	vōār ayr dayr ehn oafernlee tehlerfōānboaks
May I use your phone?	**Må jeg låne Deres telefon?**	maw yigh lawner dayrerss tehlerfōān
Can you help me get this number?	**Vil De hjælpe mig med at få dette nummer?**	veel dee yehlper migh maydh aht faw dehder noommerr
Could you change this for 25-øre coins.	**Kan De veksle denne til 25-ører?**	kehn yigh vayksler dehner til 25-ūrrerr
Do you have change for the telephone?	**Har De vekselpenge til telefonen?**	haar dee vaykserlpaynger til tehlerfōānern

Operator

Do you speak English?	**Taler De engelsk?**	tailerr dee ehngerlsk
Good morning, I want Odense 12 34 56.	**Goddag. Jeg vil gerne have Odense 12 34 56.**	goadhdai. yigh veel gehrner hæ oadhernsser 12 34 56

Note: Numbers are given in pairs.

Can I dial direct?	**Kan jeg dreje direkte?**	kehn yigh drigher dee-raykter
I want to place a personal (person-to-person) call.	**Jeg vil gerne bestille en personlig samtale.**	yigh veel gehrner bersteeler ehn payrsōānlee sahmtaaler
I want to reverse the charges.	**Modtageren betaler.**	moadhtaaerrern bertaalerr
Will you tell me the cost of the call afterwards?	**Vil De sige mig prisen på samtalen bagefter?**	veel dee sēēer migh prēēssern paw sahmtaalern bahehfterr

FOR NUMBERS, see page 175

TELEPHONE

Speaking

Hello. This is… speaking.	**Goddag. Det er…**	goadhdai. day ayr
I want to speak to…	**Jeg vil gerne tale med…**	yigh veel **gehrner tailer** maydh
Would you put me through to…?	**Vil De stille mig om til…?**	veel dee **stiler** migh oam til
I want extension…	**Jeg vil gerne have lokal…**	yigh veel **gehrner hæ** loakaal
Is that…?	**Er det…?**	ayr day

Bad luck

Would you please try again later?	**Kunne De prøve igen senere?**	kooner dee **prūr°°er** eeggayn **saynerrer**
Operator, you gave me the wrong number.	**De har givet mig forkert nummer.**	dee haar **gēēert** migh forkehrt **noommerr**
Operator, we were cut off.	**Vi er blevet afbrudt.**	vee ayr **blehert** owbroot
Would you please try the number again?	**Vær venlig at prøve nummeret igen.**	vær **vehnlee** aht **prūr°°er** noommerrert eeggayn

Telephone alphabet

A	**Anna**	ænah	P	**Peter**	pāyterr
B	**Bernhard**	bærnhaard	Q	**Quintus**	kveenturs
C	**Cecilia**	sersēēleeah	R	**Rasmus**	rahsmurs
D	**David**	dæveedh	S	**Søren**	surrern
E	**Erik**	āyreek	T	**Theodor**	tāyodoar
F	**Frederik**	frehdherreek	U	**Ulla**	oolah
G	**Georg**	gayoa	V	**Viggo**	viggo
H	**Hans**	hainss	W	**William**	veeleeam
I	**Ida**	ēēdah	X	**Xerxes**	sayrsays
J	**Johan**	yōahahn	Y	**Yrsa**	ewrsah
K	**Karen**	kaarern	Z	**Zacharias**	sahkahrēēahs
L	**Ludvig**	lewdhvee	Æ	**Ægir**	æggeer
M	**Marie**	maarēēe	Ø	**Øresund**	ūrersurn
N	**Nikolaj**	neekolaaj	Å	**Åse**	awser
O	**Odin**	ōādeen			

FOR NUMBERS see page 17.

Not there

When will he/she be back?	**Hvornår kommer han/hun tilbage?**	vor**nawr koam**err hahn/ hoon til**baa**er
Will you tell him/ her I called? My name's...	**Vil De sige til ham/ hende, at jeg har ringet. Mit navn er...**	veel dee **see**er til hahm/ **heh**ner aht yigh haar **ring**ert. meet nown ayr
Would you ask him/ her to call me?	**Vil De bede ham/ hende ringe til mig?**	veel dee **bay** hahm/ **heh**ner **ring**er til migh
Would you please take a message?	**Vil De tage imod en besked?**	veel dee tæ **ee**moadh ehn beh**skehdh**

Charges

What was the cost of that call?	**Hvad koster denne samtale?**	vahdh **koast**err **deh**ner **sahm**taaler
I want to pay for the call.	**Jeg vil gerne betale for samtalen.**	yigh veel **gehr**ner ber**taal**er foar **sahm**taalern

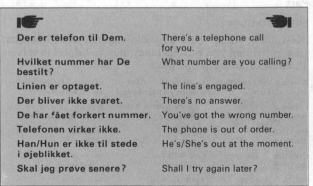

Der er telefon til Dem.	There's a telephone call for you.
Hvilket nummer har De bestilt?	What number are you calling?
Linien er optaget.	The line's engaged.
Der bliver ikke svaret.	There's no answer.
De har fået forkert nummer.	You've got the wrong number.
Telefonen virker ikke.	The phone is out of order.
Han/Hun er ikke til stede i øjeblikket.	He's/She's out at the moment.
Skal jeg prøve senere?	Shall I try again later?

TELEPHONE

The car

This section is entirely devoted to motoring. It's been divided into three parts:

Part A (pages 142–145) contains the phrases that you'll need most often at the filling station and when asking the way on the road or in town.

Part B (pages 146–149) contains general advice on motoring in Denmark, hints and regulations. It's essentially for reference, and is therefore to be browsed over, preferably in advance.

Part C (pages 150–159) is concerned with the practical details of breakdown and accidents. It includes a list of car parts and of the things that may go wrong with them. All you have to do is to show the list to the mechanic and get him to point to the repairs and items required.

Part A

Filling stations

Most filling stations don't handle major repairs, but apart from providing you with fuel they may be helpful in solving all kinds of minor problems.

Where's the nearest filling station?	**Hvor er den nær-meste benzintank?**	vōar ayr dehn **nǣr**merster bayns**ēēn**tahnk
I want...litres of petrol (gas), please.	**Jeg vil gerne have ...liter benzin.**	yigh veel **gehr**ner hæ ...leederr bayns**ēēn**
standard premium	**normal super**	noarmaal sōōberr
Give me ... crowns worth of...	**Giv mig for ...kroner...**	gee migh foar ... krōānerr
Full tank, please.	**Fyld op, tak!**	fewl op tæk

FOR NUMBERS, see page 175

Please check the oil and water.	**Vær venlig at kontrollere olie og vand.**	vær **vehn**lee aht koantroal**ay**rer **oal**yer oa vahn
Give me half a litre of oil.	**Giv mig en halv liter olie.**	gee migh ehn hahl **leeder oal**yer
Check the brake fluid.	**Vær venlig at kontrollere bremsevæsken.**	vær **vehn**lee aht koantroal**ay**rer **braym**servehskern
Fill up the battery with distilled water.	**Vær venlig at hælde destilleret vand på batteriet.**	vær **vehn**lee aht hailer dehsteel**ehr**rert vahn paw bahderr**ee**ert
Put in some anti-freeze, please.	**Vær venlig at fylde noget anti-frostvæske på.**	vær **vehn**lee aht **fewler** n**o**ert ahntee-froast-**vehs**ker paw

Fluid measures					
litres	imp. gal.	U.S. gal.	litres	imp. gal.	U.S. gal.
5	1.1	1.3	30	6.6	7.8
10	2.2	2.6	35	7.7	9.1
15	3.3	3.9	40	8.8	10.4
20	4.4	5.2	45	9.9	11.7
25	5.5	6.5	50	11.0	13.0

Can you mend this puncture (fix this flat)?	**Kan De reparere dette punkterede dæk?**	kehn dee raypahr**ay**rer **deh**der poonkt**ay**rerdher dehk
Would you please change this tire?	**Vil De udskifte dette dæk?**	veel dee **oo**dhskeefter **deh**der dehk
Would you check the tires?	**Vil De kontrollere trykket i dækkene?**	veel dee koantroal**ay**rer **trew**ggert ee **dehg**gerner
Please check the spare tire, too.	**Vær venlig også at kontrollere reservehjulet.**	vær **vehn**lee **os**saw aht koantroal**ay**rer rayss**ay**rver-y**oo**lert
1.6 front, 1.8 rear.*	**1,6 på forhjulene, 1,8 på baghjulene**	1 **kom**ah 6 paw **foar**-y**oo**lerner 1 **kom**ah 8 paw **bow**y**oo**lerner

* In Denmark the tire pressure is usually measured in kilograms per square centimetre. The conversion chart on the next page will make sure your tires get the treatment they deserve. Just point to the pressures required.

Tire pressure			
lb./sq. in.	kg/cm²	lb./sq. in.	kg/cm²
10	0.7	26	1.8
12	0.8	27	1.9
15	1.1	28	2.0
18	1.3	30	2.1
20	1.4	33	2.3
21	1.5	36	2.5
23	1.6	38	2.7
24	1.7	40	2.8

Would you clean the windscreen (windshield)?	**Vil De vaske forruden?**	veel dee **vah**sker forr**ōō**dhern
I want maintenance and lubrication service.	**Jeg vil gerne have bilen efterset og smurt.**	yigh veel **gehr**ner hæ **bēē**lern **ehf**terrseht oa sm**ōō**rt
Have you a road map of this district?	**Har De et vejkort over denne egn?**	haar dee eht **vigh**koart o°°er **deh**ner ighn
I've run out of petrol (gas) at... Could you please help me?	**Jeg er løbet tør for benzin ved... Kan De hjælpe mig?**	yigh ayr l**ūr**bert turr foar bayn**sēēn** vaydh... kehn dee **yehl**per migh

Asking the way—Street directions

Asking the way of someone in a language you don't know very well, if at all, can be a very frustrating experience. In large cities you might get to where you're going more quickly if you can produce a street plan and have somebody point out the way to go. However, here are some questions you will find useful:

Excuse me. Do you speak English?	**Undskyld, taler De engelsk?**	**oon**skewl **tail**err dee **ehng**erlsk
Can you tell me the way to...?	**Kan De sige mig vejen til...?**	kehn dee **sēē**er migh **vigh**ern til
Where's...?	**Hvor er...?**	v**ōā**r ayr
Where does this road lead to?	**Hvor fører denne vej hen?**	v**ōā**r f**ū**rrer **deh**ner vigh hayn

Are we on the right road for...?	**Er vi på rette vej til...?**	ayr vee paw **rayd**er vigh til
How far is the next village?	**Hvor langt er der til næste by?**	vōar lahngt ayr dayr til **neh**ster bew
How far is it to... from here?	**Hvor langt er der til...herfra?**	vōar lahngt ayr dayr til...hayr**fraa**

Miles into kilometres										
1 mile = 1.609 kilometres (km)										
miles	10	20	30	40	50	60	70	80	90	100
km	16	32	48	64	80	97	113	129	145	161

Kilometres into miles													
1 kilometre (km = 0.62 miles)													
km	10	20	30	40	50	60	70	80	90	100	110	120	130
miles	6	12	19	25	31	37	44	50	56	62	68	75	81

Can you tell me where...is?	**Kan De sige mig hvor...er?**	kehn dee **sēē**er migh vōar...ayr
Where can I find this address?	**Hvor kan jeg finde denne adresse?**	vōar kehn yigh **finn**er **dehn**er ah**drays**ser
Where is this?	**Hvor er dette?**	vōar ayr **deh**der
Can you show me on the map where I am?	**Kan De vise mig på kortet, hvor jeg er?**	kehn dee **vēēs**ser migh paw **koart**ert vōar yigh ayr
Can you show me on the map where... is?	**Kan De vise mig på kortet, hvor... er?**	kehn dee **vēēs**ser migh paw **koart**ert vōar...ayr
Can I park there?	**Kan jeg parkere der?**	kehn yigh pahr**kāy**rer dayr
Is that a one-way street?	**Er det en ensrettet gade?**	ayr day **ehns**rehdert **gaid**her
Does the traffic go this way?	**Er det færdsels- retningen?**	ayr day **fær**sserls- **rayt**neengern

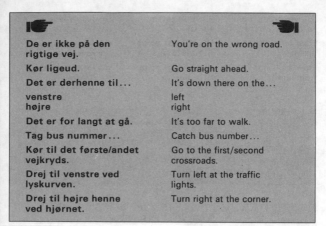

De er ikke på den rigtige vej.	You're on the wrong road.
Kør ligeud.	Go straight ahead.
Det er derhenne til...	It's down there on the...
venstre	left
højre	right
Det er for langt at gå.	It's too far to walk.
Tag bus nummer...	Catch bus number...
Kør til det første/andet vejkryds.	Go to the first/second crossroads.
Drej til venstre ved lyskurven.	Turn left at the traffic lights.
Drej til højre henne ved hjørnet.	Turn right at the corner.

Part B

Customs—Documentation

You will require the following documents to enter Denmark:

    passport
    international insurance certificate (Green Card)*
    registration (log) book
    valid home driving licence or international driving licence

The nationality plate or sticker must be on the car.

Here's my...	Her er...	hayr ayr
(international) driving licence	mit (internationale) førerbevis	meet (internaasyoanaaler) fūrrerrbehvēēss
log book (registration card)	min indregistre-ringsattest	mēēn inrayggeestrāy-reengsahtayst
passport	mit pas	meet pahss

---

* The Green Card has largely been scrapped within the EEC and Scandinavian countries. Check with your insurance company before departure.

I've nothing to declare.	**Jeg har ikke noget at deklarere.**	yigh haar igger nōaert aht dehklahrāyrer
I've...	**Jeg har...**	yigh haar
a carton of cigarettes	**et karton cigaretter**	eht kahrtong siggahrayderr
a bottle of whisky	**en flaske whisky**	ehn **flahsker** "whisky"
a bottle of wine	**en flaske vin**	ehn **flahsker** vēēn
We're staying for...	**Vi bliver...**	vee blēēerr
a week	**en uge**	ehn ōōer
two weeks	**to uger**	toa ōōerr
a month	**en måned**	ehn mawnerdh

You should have a red warning triangle for use in case of breakdown. Seat belts are compulsory for front-seat passengers. Motorcycle and scooter drivers should always wear helmets.

Driving

Denmark is covered with a network of very good roads, whether you are in the neighbourhood of Copenhagen or in the romantic byways of Jutland or one of the many islands. The motorways (expressways) are excellently engineered, and other roads are practically always surfaced.

Hovedvej (ho°°erdhvigh)	First-class main road
Landevej (lahnervigh)	Second-class road
Bivej (beevigh)	Third-class road

In Denmark, drive on the right and pass on the left.

Speed limits are 100 km/h (62 mph) on motorways (expressways), 80 km/h (50 mph) on other roads and 50 km/h (31 mph) in built-up areas unless other speeds are indicated by road signs. In the absence of any indications, priority at intersections is given to traffic coming from the right.

Cyclists are accorded special treatment throughout the country, with special cycle paths bordering many of the main

CAR – INFORMATION

roads (with the exception of motorways). Motorists should be careful not to infringe on the rights of these two-wheeled commuters whom they will encounter in great numbers!

Ferries between the mainland and the islands are frequent and efficient, but reserve space in advance during the summer months and the other holiday periods. You drive yourself on and off the boat with a minimum of fuss.

You will find Danish drivers courteous and considerate, even-tempered and helpful to foreigners in difficulties. They tend to switch on their lights at the slightest hint of fog or murky weather and also when driving with the sun behind them, for the benefit of oncoming traffic.

The police are normally quite lenient with tourists, but don't push your luck too far. For small offenses you can be fined on the spot.

I'm sorry. I don't speak much Danish.	**Undskyld, men jeg taler ikke ret meget dansk.**	oonskewl mayn yigh tailerr igger rayt mighert dahnsk
How much is the fine?	**Hvor meget skal jeg betale i bøde?**	vōar mighert skahl yigh bertaaler ee būrdher

Parking

Major towns have parking meters and zones where parking is limited. Parking discs (*parkeringsskive*—pahr**kāy**rings-sk**ēē**ver) can be obtained free from police stations, garages, post offices and most banks.

Excuse me. May I park here?	**Undskyld. Kan jeg parkere her?**	oonskewl. kehn yigh pahr**kāy**rer hayr
How long may I park here?	**Hvor længe kan jeg parkere her?**	vōar lainger kehn yigh pahr**kāy**rer hayr
What's the charge for parking here?	**Hvad koster det at parkere her?**	vahdh **koast**err day aht pahr**kāy**rer hayr
Excuse me. Do you have some change for the parking meter?	**Undskyld. Har de småpenge til parko-metret?**	oonskewl. haar dee **smaw**paynger till pahrkoa**māy**trert

Danish road signs

Road signs are practically standardized throughout western Europe. Those shown on pages 160 and 161 are the most important ones.

In addition, Denmark uses some signs and notices of its own, sometimes in conjuction with pictographs, sometimes alone. While driving through Denmark you're certain to encounter some of those listed below. Study this page beforehand so you're prepared for them.

BEGRÆNSET VOGNHØJDE	Height restriction
DATOPARKERING	Parking prohibited on even/odd days
ENSRETTET	One-way street
FODGÆNGERE	Pedestrians
FODGÆNGERE FORBUDT	No pedestrians
HOSPITAL	Hospital—Silence
JERNBANEOVERSKÆRING	Railway level crossing
OMKØRSEL	Diversion, detour
OPHØR AF...	End of restriction
OVERHALING FORBUDT	No overtaking
PARKERING FORBUDT	No parking
PAS PÅ	General warning notice
POLITI	Police
RABATTEN ER BLØD	Soft shoulder
RUNDKØRSEL	Roundabout (rotary)
SKOLE	School
UDKØRSEL	Exit
UJÆVN VEJ	Bad road
VEJARBEJDE	Road works
FALCK-ZONEN	24-hour telephone stations for emergencies, breakdown, accident

Note that emergency telephone call boxes are located at frequent intervals along Danish motorways (freeways).

Part C

Accidents

This section is confined to immediate aid. The legal problems of responsibility and settlement can be taken care of at a later stage.

Your first concern will be for the injured.

Is anyone hurt?	**Er nogen såret?**	ayr **nōaern** sawrert
Don't move.	**Rør Dem ikke.**	rūrr dehm **igger**
It's all right, don't worry.	**Det er i orden. Vær ikke bange.**	day ayr ee oardern. vær **igger bahnger**
Where's the nearest telephone?	**Hvor er den nærmeste telefon?**	vōar ayr dehn **nærmerster** tehlerfōān
Can I use your phone? There's been an accident.	**Må jeg låne Deres telefon? Der er sket en ulykke.**	maw yigh **lawner dayrerss** tehlerfōān? dayr ayr skeht ehn ōōlewgger
Call a doctor/an ambulance quickly.	**Tilkald en læge/en ambulance hurtigt.**	tilkahl ehn **laier**/ehn ahmboolahnsser hoorteet
There are people injured.	**Der er tilskade-komne.**	dayr ayr til**skaadher-** koamner
Help me get them out of the car.	**Hjælp mig med at få dem ud af bilen.**	yehlp migh maydh aht faw dehm ōōdh ah **bēēlern**

Police—Exchange of information

Please call the police.	**Vær venlig at til-kalde politiet.**	vær **vehnlee** aht til-kahler poaleet**ēēert**
There's been an accident.	**Der er sket en ulykke.**	dayr ayr skeht ehn ōōlewgger
It's about 2 kilo-metres from...	**Det er cirka 2 kilo-meter fra...**	day ayr **seerkah** 2 keeloa-**māydherr** fraa
I'm on the Europa-road 3, 25 kilometres north of Århus.	**Jeg er på E 3, 25 kilometer nord for Århus.**	yigh ayr paw ai 3, 25 keeloamāydherr nōar foar awrhōōss
Here's my name and address.	**Her er mit navn og min adresse.**	hayr ayr meet nown oa mēēn ah**draysser**
Would you mind acting as a witness?	**Har De noget imod at være vidne?**	haar dee **nōaert** eemoadh aht v**ærer veedhner**

CAR – INFORMATION

I'd like an inter- preter.	**Jeg vil gerne have en tolk.**	yigh veel **gehr**ner hæ ehn toalk

Remember to put out a red warning triangle if your car is
out of action or impeding traffic.

Breakdown

...and that's what we'll do with this section: break it down
into four phases.

1. *On the road*
   You ask where the nearest garage is.

2. *At the garage*
   You tell the mechanic what's wrong.

3. *Finding the trouble*
   He tells you what he thinks needs doing.

4. *Getting it repaired*
   You tell him to repair it and, once that's over, settle the
   account (or argue about it).

Phase 1—On the road

Where's the nearest garage?	**Hvor er det nær- meste bilværksted?**	vōār ayr day **nǣr**merster **bēēl**værkstaydh
Excuse me, my car has broken down. May I use your phone?	**Undskyld. Min vogn har fået motorstop. Må jeg låne tele- fonen?**	**oon**skewl. mēēn voan haar fawert **mōā**toarstoab. maw yigh **law**ner tehlerf**ōā**- nern
What's the telephone number of the nearest garage?	**Hvilket telefon- nummer har det nærmeste bilværk- sted?**	**vil**kert tehlerf**ōā**noommerr haar day **nǣr**merster **bēēl**værkstaydh
I've had a breakdown at...	**Jeg har fået motor- stop ved...**	yigh haar **faw**ert **mōā**toar- stoab vaydh
We're on the Europa- road 6, about 10 kilometres from Odense.	**Vi befinder os på E 6, cirka 10 km fra Odense.**	vee ber**fin**nerr oss paw ai 6 **seer**kah 10 keeloam**āy**- dherr fraa **oad**hernsser

Can you send a mechanic?	**Kan De sende en mekaniker?**	kehn dee **sayner** ehn mehkahneeggerr
Can you send a truck to tow my car?	**Kan De sende en vogn til at tage min bil på slæb?**	kehn dee **sayner** ehn voan til aht tæ mēen bēel paw slehb
How long will you be?	**Hvor lang tid vil det vare, før De kommer?**	vōar lang teedh veel day **vǣ**rer fūrr dee **koam**err

Phase 2—At the garage

<table>
<tr><td>Can you help me?</td><td>Kan De hjælpe mig?</td><td>kehn dee yehlper migh</td></tr>
<tr><td>I don't know what's wrong with it.</td><td>Jeg ved ikke, hvad der er i vejen.</td><td>yigh vehdh igger vahdh dayr ayr ee vighern</td></tr>
<tr><td>I think there's something wrong with the...</td><td>Jeg tror, der er noget i vejen med...</td><td>yigh troar dayr ayr nōaert ee vighern maydh ee vighern maydh</td></tr>
<tr><td>acceleration</td><td>accelerationen</td><td>ahksehlerrahsyoanern</td></tr>
<tr><td>air conditioning</td><td>ventilationen</td><td>vaynteelahsyoanern</td></tr>
<tr><td>axle</td><td>akslen</td><td>ahkslern</td></tr>
<tr><td>battery</td><td>batteriet</td><td>bahderrēēert</td></tr>
<tr><td>brakes</td><td>bremserne</td><td>braymsserner</td></tr>
<tr><td>choke</td><td>chokeren</td><td>shoaggerrern</td></tr>
<tr><td>clutch</td><td>koblingen</td><td>koableengern</td></tr>
<tr><td>cooling system</td><td>køleren</td><td>kūrlerrern</td></tr>
<tr><td>dip (dimmer) switch</td><td>nedblændingskontakten</td><td>nǣydhblaineengskoantahktern</td></tr>
<tr><td>direction indicator</td><td>blinklyset</td><td>blinklewssert</td></tr>
<tr><td>distributor</td><td>strømfordeleren</td><td>strurmfordǣylerrern</td></tr>
<tr><td>door</td><td>døren</td><td>durrern</td></tr>
<tr><td>dynamo</td><td>dynamoen</td><td>dewnaamoaern</td></tr>
<tr><td>electrical system</td><td>det elektriske system</td><td>day ehlayktreesker sewstehm</td></tr>
<tr><td>engine</td><td>motoren</td><td>mōatoarern</td></tr>
<tr><td>exhaust system</td><td>udstødningen</td><td>ōōdhsturdneengern</td></tr>
<tr><td>fan</td><td>ventilatoren</td><td>vaynteelahtoarern</td></tr>
<tr><td>fan belt</td><td>ventilatorremmen</td><td>vaynteelahtoarraymern</td></tr>
<tr><td>fuel feed</td><td>benzintilførslen</td><td>baynsēēntilfūrrslern</td></tr>
<tr><td>gears</td><td>gearene</td><td>gēēerner</td></tr>
<tr><td>generator</td><td>dynamoen</td><td>dewnaamoaern</td></tr>
<tr><td>heating</td><td>varmesystemet</td><td>vahrmersewstehmert</td></tr>
<tr><td>horn</td><td>hornet</td><td>hoarnert</td></tr>
<tr><td>ignition system</td><td>tændingen</td><td>tehneengern</td></tr>
<tr><td>injection system</td><td>tilførselssystemet</td><td>tilfūrrserlssewstǣymert</td></tr>
</table>

lights	lygterne	lewgterrner
brake lights	stoplygterne	stoablewgterrner
headlights	forlygterne	foarlewgterrner
rear (tail) lights	baglygterne	bowlewgterrner
reversing lights (backup)	baklygterne	bahklewgterrner
muffler	lydpotten	lewdhpoadern
oil system	smøresystemet	smurrersewstaymert
overdrive	overgearet	o°°ergeeerert
radiator	køleren	kūrlerrern
seat	sædet	saidhert
seat belt	sikkerhedsselen	siggerrhehdssehlern
silencer	lydpotten	lewdhpoadern
speedometer	speedometeret	speedoamayderrert
starter motor	startermotoren	stahrterrmoātoaern
steering	styretøjet	stewrertoiert
suspension	affjedringen	owfyehdreengern
transmission	transmissionen	trahnsmeesyoanern
turn signal	blinklyset	bleenklewssert
wheels	hjulene	yōōlerner
wipers	vinduesviskerne	veendōōssveeskerrner

LEFT	RIGHT	FRONT	BACK
TIL VENSTRE	**TIL HØJRE**	**FOR**	**BAG**
(til **vayn**strer)	(til **hoi**rer)	(foar)	(bah)

It's...

backfiring	tændingsfejl	tehneengssfighl
blown	sprængt	sprehngt
broken	i stykker	ee stewggerr
burnt	brændt ud	brehnt ōōdh
chafing	gnaver	gnower
cracked	revnet	reh°°nert
defective	defekt	dehfaykt
disconnected	gået løs	gawert lurss
dry	tør	turr
frozen	frosset	froassert
jammed	blokeret	bloakayrert
jerking	støder	stūrdherr
knocking	banker	bahngkerr

CAR – REPAIRS

leaking	**læk**	lehk
loose	**løs**	lurss
noisy	**støjer**	stoierr
overheating	**for varm**	foar vahrm
slack	**slap**	slahp
slipping	**glider/løsner sig**	gleedherr/lursnerr sigh
split	**spaltet**	spahltert
stuck	**sidder fast**	seedherr fahst
vibrating	**vibrerer**	veebrayrerr
weak	**svag**	svaa

The car won't start.	**Bilen vil ikke starte.**	beelern veel igger stahrter
The car won't pull.	**Bilen trækker ikke.**	beelern trehgger igger
The car is making a funny noise.	**Bilen laver en mærkelig støj.**	beelern lahverr ehn mærkerlee stoi
It's locked and the keys are inside.	**Den er låst, og nøglerne ligger indeni.**	dehn ayr lawst oa noilerrner liggerr innernee
The radiator is leaking.	**Køleren lækker.**	kurlerren lehgger
The clutch engages too quickly.	**Koblingen har ikke frigang nok.**	koableengern haar igger freegahng noak
I can't engage first/reverse gear.	**Jeg kan ikke sætte den i første gear/bakgear.**	yigh kehn igger saider dehn ee furrster geer/bahkgeer
The steering wheel's vibrating.	**Rattet vibrerer.**	rahdert veebrayrerr
The suspension is weak.	**Affjedringen er svag.**	owfyaydhreengern ayr svaa
The...needs adjusting.	**...skal justeres.**	...skahl yoostehrerss
brake/clutch/idling	**bremserne/koblingen/tomgangen**	braymsserner/koableengern/toamgahngern

Now that you've explained what's wrong, you'll want to know how long it'll take to repair it and make your arrangements accordingly.

How long will it take to find out what's wrong?	**Hvor lang tid tager det at finde ud af, hvad der er i vejen?**	voar lahng teedh taar day aht finner oodh ah vahdh dayr ayr ee vighern
How long will it take to repair?	**Hvor lang tid tager det at reparere det?**	voar lahng teedh taar day aht raypahrayrer dehn

CAR – REPAIRS

Can you give me a lift into town?	**Kan De tage mig med til byen?**	kehn dee tæ migh maydh til bēwern
Is there a place to stay nearby?	**Er der et opholds- sted i nærheden?**	ayr dayr eht ophoals- staydh ee nǣr- hehdhern
May I use your phone?	**Må jeg låne Deres telefon?**	maw yigh lawner dayrerss tehlerfōān

Phase 3—Finding the trouble

Now it's up to the mechanic to pinpoint the trouble and repair it. Just hand him the book and point to the text in Danish below.

Vær venlig at se på denne alfabetiske liste og peg på, hvad De tror er galt. Hvis Deres kunde ønsker at vide, hvad der er i vejen, vær venlig at bruge det udtryk, der passer i næste liste ("i stykker", kortsluttet, osv.). *

affjedringen	suspension
akkumulatorvæsken	battery fluid
akslen	shaft
batteriet	battery
belægningen	lining
benzinmåleren	fuel gauge
benzinpumpen	fuel pump
benzintanken	fuel tank
benzintilførslen	fuel feed
blandingen	mixture
bolten	bolt
bremsen	brake
bremsebelægningen	brake lining
bremseskoene	shoes
bremsetromlen	brake drum
bundkarret	sump (oil pan)
børsterne	brushes
chokeren	choke
cylinderen	cylinder
differentialet	differential
dynamoen	dynamo (generator)
det elektriske system	electrical system
fjederen	spring
forbindelsen	connection

* Please look at the following alphabetical list and point to the defective item. If your customer wants to know what's wrong with it, pick the applicable term from the next list (broken, short-circuited, etc.).

CAR – REPAIRS

forbindelses (stempel)-stangen	connecting (piston) rod
gearkassen	gear box
gearstangen	gear lever
hjulene	wheels
hovedlejerne	main bearings
det hydrauliske bremsesystem	hydraulic brake system
kardanakslen	propeller shaft
kardanleddene	universal joint
knastakslen	camshaft
koblingen	clutch
koblingspedalen	clutch pedal
koblingspladen	clutch plate
kondensatoren	condenser
kontrollampen	warning lamp
krumtapakslen	crankshaft
krumtaphuset	crankcase
kullene	brushes
køleren	radiator
kølesystemet	cooling system
led(pakningen)	joint (packing)
ledningen	cable
ledningerne	leads, wiring
luftfiltret	air filter
lydpotten	silencer (muffler)
membranen	diaphragm
monteringerne	mountings
motorblokken	block
motoren	engine
måleren	gauge
nedblændingskontakten	dip (dimmer) switch
oliefiltret	oil filter
oliekøleren	oil cooler
oliepumpen	oil pump
overtrækket	casing
platinstifterne	points
pumpen	pump
ratsøjlen	steering column (post)
reflektorerne	reflector
relæet	relay
spolen	coil
sporingen	tracking
stabilisatoren	stabilizer
starteren	starter motor
starterens anker	starter armature

stempelringene	rings
stemplet	piston
strømfordeleren	distributor
strømfordelerledningerne	distributor leads
styrehuset	steering box
styretøjet	steering
støddæmperen	shock-absorber
svinghjulet	flywheel
svømmeren	float
tandstangsstyrehuset	rack and pinion
termostaten	thermostat
tilførselspumpen	injection pump
toppakningen	cylinder head gasket
topstykket	cylinder head
transmissionen	relay, transmission
tænderne	teeth
tændingen	timing, ignition
tændrørene	sparking plugs
tændspolen	ignition coil
udstødningspakningen	manifold gasket
udstødningsrøret	manifold
vandpumpen	water pump
ventilatoren	fan
ventilatorremmen	fan belt
ventilen	valve
ventilløfteren	tappet
vingehjulsstangen	rotor arm

Den følgende liste indeholder ord, der udtrykker hvad der er i vejen, eller hvad der skal gøres ved bilen.*

at balancere	to balance
at afmontere	to strip down
angrebet	corroded
binder	jammed
brændt	burnt
defekt	defective
at forny belægningen	to reline
frosset	frozen
glider	slipping
er hullet	pitted
hurtig	quick
høj	high

* The following list contains words which describe what's wrong as well as what may need to be done.

i stykker	broken
at justere	to adjust
klemmer	jammed
lav	low
er læk	leaking
løber varm	overheating
løs/slap	loose
at løsne	to loosen
løsrevet	disconnected
at oplade	to charge
oplader ikke	not charging
opslidt	worn
overgang	short-circuited
at rense	to clean
revnet	cracked
rig	rich
slap	loose
slibe til	to grind in
har slør	slack
snavset	dirty
har spil	play
sprunget	blown, broken
starter ikke	misfiring
at stramme	to tighten
svag	weak
tør	dry
at udlufte	to bleed
at udskifte	to change, replace

Phase 4—Getting it repaired

Have you found the trouble?	**Har De fundet ud af, hvad der er i vejen?**	haar dee foonnert ōōdh ah vahdh dayr ayr ee vighern
Is that serious?	**Er det alvorligt?**	ayr day ahlvoārleet
Can you repair it?	**Kan De ordne det?**	kehn dee oardner day
Can you do it now?	**Kan De gøre det nu?**	kehn dee gūrrer day noo
What's it going to cost?	**Hvad vil det koste?**	vahdh veel day koaster

What if he says "no"?

Why can't you do it?	**Hvorfor kan De ikke gøre det?**	**vor**for kehn dee **igger** **gū**rrer day
Is it essential to have that part?	**Er det absolut nødvendigt med den del?**	ayr day **ahb**soaloot nurdh**vaynd**eet maydh dehn dayl

How long is it going to take to get the spare parts?	**Hvor lang tid vil det tage at skaffe reservedelene?**	vōār lahng teedh veel day tæ aht **skah**fer rayss**āy**rverdehlerner
Where's the nearest garage that can repair it?	**Hvor er det nærmeste værksted, der kan klare reparationen?**	vōār ayr day **næ**rmerster **værk**staydh dayr kehn **klaa**rer raypahrah-syoanern
Can you fix it so that I can get as far as...?	**Kan De ordne det, så jeg kan køre til...?**	kehn dee **oard**ner day saw yigh kehn **kū**rrer til

If you're really stuck, ask:

Can I leave my car here for a day/a few days?	**Kan jeg efterlade vognen her en dag/ i et par dage?**	kehn yigh **ehf**terrlaadher **voa**nern hayr ehn dai/ ee eht pahr **dai**er

Settling the bill

Is everything fixed?	**Er alt blevet repareret?**	ayr ahlt **blay**vert ray-·pahr**āy**rert
How much do I owe you?	**Hvor meget skylder jeg Dem?**	vōār **migh**ert **skew**lerr yigh dehm
Will you take a traveller's cheque?	**Tager De imod rejsechecks?**	taar dee ee**moa**dh **righss**erchayks
Thanks very much for your help.	**Mange tak for Deres hjælp.**	**mahn**ger tæk foar **day**rerss yehlp
This is for you.	**Værsågod, det er til Dem.**	**vær**sawgoadh day ayr til dehm

CAR – REPAIRS

But you may feel that the workmanship is sloppy or that you're paying for work not done. Get the bill itemized. If necessary, get it translated before you pay.

I'd like to check the bill first. Will you itemize the work done?	**Jeg vil gerne først kontrollere regningen. Vil De specificere arbejdet?**	yigh veel **gehr**ner furst koantroal**āy**rer **righ**neenggern. veel dee spehsseefeess**āy**rer ahr-**bigh**dert

If the garage still won't back down, and you're sure you're right get the help of a third party.

Some international road signs

No vehicles

No entry

No overtaking (passing)

Oncoming traffic has priority

Maximum speed limit

No parking

Caution

Intersection

Dangerous bend (curve)

Road narrows

Intersection with secondary road

Two-way traffic

Dangerous hill

Uneven road

Falling rocks

Give way (yield)

Main road,
thoroughfare

End of restriction

One-way traffic

Traffic goes
this way

Roundabout
(rotary)

Bicycles only

Pedestrians
only

Minimum speed
limit

Keep right
(left if symbol
reversed)

Parking

Hospital

Motorway
(expressway)

Motor vehicles
only

Filling station

No through road

Doctor

Frankly, how much use is a phrase book going to be to you in case of serious injury or illness? The only phrase you need in such an emergency is...

Get a doctor, quickly!	**Skaf en læge, hurtigt!**	skahf ehn **lai**er **hoor**teet

But there are minor aches and pains, ailments and irritations that can upset the best-planned trip. Here we can help you and, perhaps, the doctor.

Some doctors will speak English well; others will know enough for your needs. But suppose there's something the doctor can't explain because of language difficulties? We've thought of that. As you'll see, this section has been arranged to enable you and the doctor to communicate. From page 165 to 171, you'll find your part of the dialogue on the upper half of each page—the doctor's is on the lower half.

The whole section has been divided into three parts: illness, wounds, nervous tension. Page 171 is concerned with prescriptions and fees.

General

Can you get me a doctor?	**Kan De skaffe en læge?**	kehn dee **skah**fer ehn **lai**er
Is there a doctor here?	**Er der en læge her?**	ayr dayr ehn **lai**er hayr
Please telephone for a doctor immediately.	**Vær venlig at ringe efter en læge straks.**	vær **vehn**lee aht **reen**ger **ehf**terr ehn **lai**er strahks
Where's there a doctor who speaks English?	**Hvor er der en læge, der taler engelsk?**	vōār ayr dayr ehn **lai**er dayr **tai**lerr **ehn**gerlsk
I'd like to contact the English/American embassy, please.	**Jeg vil gerne tale med nogen fra den engelske/amerikanske ambassade.**	yigh veel **gehr**ner **tai**ler maydh **nō̄a**ern fraa dehn **ehn**gerlsker/ahmehree**kaan**sker ahmbah**ssadh**er

FOR CHEMIST'S, see page 108

（左余白縦書き：DOCTOR）

Where's the surgery (doctor's office)?	**Hvor har lægen kon-sultation?**	vōār haar laiern koan-sooltahsyoan
Could the doctor come to see me here?	**Kan lægen komme her?**	kehn laiern koamer hayr
What time can the doctor come?	**Hvornår kan lægen være her?**	vornawr kehn laiern vǣrer hayr

Symptoms

Use this section to tell the doctor what's wrong. Basically, what he'll require to know is:

What?	(ache, pain, bruise, etc.)
Where?	(arm, stomach, etc.)
How long?	(have you had the trouble)

Before you visit the doctor find out the answers to these questions by glancing through the pages that follow. In this way, you'll save time.

Parts of the body

ankle	**anklen**	ahnklern
appendix	**blindtarmen**	bleentahrmern
arm	**armen**	ahrmern
artery	**arterien**	ahrtayrēēern
back	**ryggen**	rewggern
bladder	**blæren**	blairern
blood	**blodet**	bloadhert
bone	**knoglen**	knoalern
breast	**brystet**	brewstert
cheek	**kinden**	keenern
chest	**brystkassen**	brewstkahssern
ear	**øret**	ūrrert
elbow	**albuen**	ahlbōōern
eye	**øjet**	oiert
face	**ansigtet**	ahnseegtert
finger	**fingeren**	feengerrern
foot	**foden**	foadhern
forehead	**panden**	pahnern
gland	**kirtelen**	keertlern

hair	**håret**	hawrert
hand	**hånden**	hawnern
head	**hovedet**	ho°°erdhert
heart	**hjertet**	yairtert
heel	**hælen**	hailern
hip	**hoften**	hoaftern
intestines	**tarmene**	tahrmerner
jaw	**kæben**	kaibern
joint	**leddet**	lehdhert
kidney	**nyren**	new̄rern
knee	**knæet**	knaiert
knuckle	**knoen**	knoaern
leg	**benet**	behnert
ligament	**senebåndet**	sehnerbawnert
lip	**læben**	laibern
liver	**leveren**	lāȳverrern
lung	**lungen**	loongern
mouth	**munden**	moonnern
muscle	**musklen**	moosklern
neck	**nakken**	nahggern
nerve	**nerven**	nayrvern
nervous system	**nervesystemet**	nayrversewstāȳmert
nose	**næsen**	naissern
pelvis	**bækkenet**	behggernert
rectum	**endetarmen**	aynertahrmern
rib	**ribbenet**	reebehnert
shoulder	**skulderen**	skoolerrern
sinus	**bihulen**	beehōōlern
skin	**huden**	hōōdhern
spine	**rygraden**	rewgrahdhen
stomach	**maven**	maavern
tendon	**senen**	sāȳnern
throat	**halsen**	hahlssern
thumb	**tommelfingeren**	toamerlfeengerrern
toe	**tåen**	tawern
tongue	**tungen**	toongern
tonsils	**mandlerne**	mahnlehrner
urine	**urinen**	oorēēnern
vein	**venen**	vehnern
wrist	**håndleddet**	hawnlehdhert

LEFT	RIGHT
VENSTRE	**HØJRE**
(vaynstrer)	(hoirer)

PATIENT

Part 1—Illness

I'm not feeling well.	**Jeg føler mig ikke godt tilpas.**	yigh **fūr**lerr migh **igger** got til**pahss**
I've got a pain here.	**Jeg har smerter her.**	yigh haar **smayr**terr hayr
My...hurts.	**Jeg har ondt i...**	yigh haar oant ee
I've/He's/She's got (a)...	**Jeg/Han/Hun har...**	yigh/hahn/hoon haar
backache	**rygsmerter**	**rewg**smayrterr
fever	**feber**	**feh**berr
headache	**hovedpine**	ho°°erdhp**ēē**ner
sore throat	**ondt i halsen**	oant ee **hahl**ssern
stomach ache	**mavepine**	**maa**verp**ēē**ner
I'm constipated	**Jeg har forstoppelse.**	yigh haar forstoab**erl**sser
I've a bad cough.	**Jeg har en slem hoste.**	yigh haar ehn slaym **hoa**ster
I've been vomiting.	**Jeg har kastet op.**	yigh haar **kahs**tert op

DOCTOR

1—Sygdomme

Hvor gør det ondt?	Where does it hurt?
Hvad slags smerte er det?	What sort of pain is it?
dump/skarp/bankende konstant/kommer og går	dull/sharp/throbbing constant/on and off
Hvor længe har De haft disse smerter?	How long have you had this pain?
Hvor længe har De følt Dem dårlig tilpas?	How long have you been feeling like this?
Smøg ærmet op.	Roll up your sleeve.
Vær venlig at klæde Dem af til bæltestedet.	Please undress to the waist.
Vær venlig at tage bukser/nederdel og underbenklæder af.	Please remove your trousers/skirt and underclothes.

DOCTOR

PATIENT

I feel...	Jeg...	yigh
dizzy	er svimmel	ayr sveemerl
faint	er dårlig	ayr dawrlee
nauseous	har kvalme	haar kvahlmer
shivery	har kuldegysninger	haar koolergewssneenger

I've/He's/She's got (a/an)...	Jeg/Han/Hun har...	yigh/hahn/hoon haar
abscess	en absces	ehn ahbsayss
asthma	astma	ahstmah
boil	en byld	ehn bewl
chill	en forkølelse	ehn forkurlersser
cold	snue	snooer
constipation	forstoppelse	forstoaberlsser
cramps	krampe	krahmper
diarrhoea	diarré	deeahray
fever	feber	fehberr
haemorrhoids	hæmorroider	haimooroaedherr
hay fever	høfeber	hurfehberr

DOCTOR

Læg Dem ned her.	Please lie down over here.
Luk munden op.	Open your mouth.
Træk vejret dybt.	Breathe deeply.
Host.	Cough, please.
Gør dette ondt?	Does this hurt?
Jeg tager Deres temperatur.	I'll take your temperature.
Er det første gang, De har det sådan?	Is this the first time you've had this?
Jeg vil gerne have en prøve af Deres urin/afføring.	I want a sample of your urine/ stools.
Hvilken blodtype har De?	What is your blood type?

DOCTOR

PATIENT

hernia	**brok**	broak
indigestion	**mavekneb**	**maa**verknehb
inflammation of...	**betændelse i...**	ber**tain**erlser ee
influenza	**influenza**	inflooāynsah
measles	**mæslinger**	**mehs**lingerr
morning sickness	**morgenubehag**	mōaernōōbehhaa
rheumatism	**reumatisme**	roimah**tees**mer
stiff neck	**nakkestivhed**	**nahg**gersteevhehdh
sunburn	**solforbrænding**	**soal**forbrehneeng
sunstroke	**solstik**	**soal**steek
tonsillitis	**betændte mandler**	ber**tain**ter mahnlerr
ulcer	**mavesår**	**maa**versawr
whooping cough	**kighoste**	**kee**hoaster

It's nothing serious, I hope?	**Det er vel ikke noget alvorligt?**	day ayr vayl **igger** nōāert ahl**vōā**rleet
I'd like you to prescribe some medicine for me.	**Jeg vil gerne have, De ordinerer mig et middel.**	yigh veel **gehr**ner hæ dee oardeen**āy**rer migh eht **meedh**erl

---

DOCTOR

De skal ikke være foruroliget.	It's nothing to worry about.
De skal holde sengen i... dage.	You must stay in bed for... days.
De er/har...	You've got (a/an)...
betændelse i.../blindtarmsbetændelse/forkølet/ ledegigt/lungebetændelse/ madforgiftning/mavesår	inflammation of.../appendicitis/ cold/arthritis/pneumonia/ food poisoning/ulcer
De er overtræt. De har brug for hvile.	You're over-tired. You need a rest.
De bør undersøges af en specialist.	I want you to see a specialist.
De skal indlægges på hospitalet til undersøgelse.	I want you to go to the hospital for an examination.
Jeg skriver recept på nogle antibiotica.	I'll prescribe an antibiotic.

DOCTOR

PATIENT

I'm a diabetic.	**Jeg har sukkersyge.**	yigh haar sooggerrsēwer
I've a cardiac condition.	**Jeg har en hjerte-sygdom.**	yigh haar ehn yairter-sēwdoam
I had a heart attack in...	**Jeg havde et hjerte-anfald i...**	yigh howdher eht yairter-ahnfahl ee
I'm allergic to...	**Jeg er allergisk mod...**	yigh ayr ahlāyrgeesk moadh
This is my usual medicine.	**Her er min sæd-vanlige medicin.**	hayr ayr mēen sehdhvaan-lēēer mehdeessēēn
I need this medicine.	**Jeg har brug for denne medicin.**	yigh haar broo foar dehner mehdeessēēn
I'm expecting a baby.	**Jeg venter et barn.**	yigh vaynterr eht bahrn
Can I travel?	**Kan jeg rejse?**	kehn yigh righsser

DOCTOR

Hvor stor dosis insulin tager De?	What dose of insulin are you taking?
Indsprøjtninger eller piller?	Injection or oral?
Hvilken behandling har De hidtil fået?	What treatment have you been having?
Hvilken medicin har De hidtil taget?	What medicine have you been taking?
Har De nogensinde haft bi-virkninger fra penicillin?	Have you ever had ill effects from penicillin?
De har haft et (let) hjerteanfald.	You've had a (slight) heart attack.
Vi bruger ikke...i Danmark. Dette er et tilsvarende middel.	We don't use...in Denmark. This is very similar.
Hvornår skal barnet komme?	When's the baby due?
De må ikke rejse før...	You can't travel until...

PATIENT

Part 2—Wounds

Could you have a look at this...?	**Vil De se på...**	veel dee say paw
blister	**denne blære/vable**	dehner blairer/vaabler
boil	**denne byld**	dehner bewl
bruise	**denne kvæstelse**	dehner kvehsterlsser
burn	**denne forbrænding**	dehner forbrehneeng
cut	**dette snitsår**	dehder sneetsawr
graze	**denne hud-afskrabning**	dehder hōōdhowskrahb-neeng
insect bite	**dette insektstik**	dehder insayktsteek
lump	**denne bule**	dehner bōōler
rash	**dette udslæt**	dehder ōōdhsleht
swelling	**denne hævelse**	dehner haiverlsser
wound	**dette sår**	dehder sawr
I can't move my... It hurts.	**Jeg kan ikke bevæge... Det gør ondt.**	yigh kehn igger bervaier ...day gurr oant

---

DOCTOR

2—Sår

Det er (ikke) inficeret.	It's (not) infected.
De har en diskosprolaps.	You've got a slipped disc.
Hvornår blev De sidst røntgen-fotograferet?	When were you last x-rayed?
De skal røntgenfotograferes.	I want you to have an x-ray.
Er De blevet vaccineret mod stivkrampe? Hvornår?	Have you been vaccinated against tetanus? When?
Den/det er...	It's...
brækket/forstuvet forvredet/bristet	broken/sprained dislocated/torn
De har forstrakt en muskel.	You've pulled a muscle.
Jeg giver Dem et antiseptisk middel. Det er ikke alvorligt.	I'll give you an antiseptic. It's not serious.
De skal komme til kontrol igen om...dage.	I want you to come and see me in...days' time.

DOCTOR

PATIENT

Part 3—Nervous tension

I'm in a nervous state.	**Jeg er meget nervøs.**	yigh ayr **might**ert nayrv**ūrss**
I'm feeling depressed.	**Jeg føler mig deprimeret.**	yigh **fūr**lerr migh dehpreem**ayr**ert
I want some sleeping pills.	**Jeg vil gerne have nogle sovepiller.**	yigh veel **gehr**ner hæ **nōā**ler so°°erpeelerr
I can't eat.	**Jeg kan ikke spise.**	yigh kehn **igg**er sp**ēē**sser
I can't sleep.	**Jeg kan ikke sove.**	yigh kehn **igg**er so°°er
I'm having nightmares.	**Jeg har mareridt.**	yigh haar **maar**erreet
Can you prescribe a/an...?	**Kan De ordinere...?**	kehn dee oardeen**ay**rer
tranquillizer	**et beroligende middel**	eht behroal**ēē**erner **meed**herl
anti-depressant	**et opkvikkende middel**	eht opkveeggerner **meed**herl

DOCTOR

DOCTOR

3—Nervøse lidelser

De lider af nervøsitet.	You're suffering from nervous tension.
De skal have ro.	You need a rest.
Hvilke piller har De taget?	What medicine have you been taking?
Hvor mange om dagen?	How many a day?
Hvor længe har De haft det sådan?	How long have you been feeling like this?
Jeg skriver recept på et middel.	I'll prescribe some medicine.
Jeg skal give Dem et beroligende middel.	I'll give you a tranquillizer.

PATIENT

Prescriptions and dosage

What kind of medicine is this?	**Hvad slags medicin er dette her?**	vahdh slahgss mehdeess_ēēn_ ayr **deh**der hayr
How many times a day should I take it?	**Hvor mange gange skal jeg tage det daglig?**	v_ōā_r **mahng**er **gahng**er skahl yigh tæ day **dow**leet
Must I swallow them whole?	**Skal jege sluge dem hele?**	skahl yigh sl_ōō_er dehm **heh**ler

Fee

How much do I owe you?	**Hvad skylder jeg Dem?**	vahdh **skew**lerr yigh dehm
Do I pay you now or will you send me your bill?	**Skal jeg betale nu eller sender De mig regningen?**	skahl yigh beh**taa**ler noo **ehl**err **say**nerr dee migh **righ**neengern
May I have a receipt?	**Kan jeg få en kvittering?**	kehn yigh faw ehn kvee-**tāy**reeng
Thanks for your help, Doctor.	**Mange tak for Deres hjælp.**	**mahng**er tæk foar **dayr**erss yehlp

DOCTOR

Recepter og dosering

Tag...teskefulde af denne medicin hver...time.	Take...teaspoons of this medicine every...hours.
Tag...piller med et glas vand...	Take...pills with a glass of water....
...gange daglig	...times a day
før hvert måltid	before each meal
efter hvert måltid	after each meal
mellem måltiderne	between meals
om morgenen	in the morning
om aftenen	at night

Honoraret

Det bliver... kroner, tak.	That's... crowns, please.
Vær venlig at betale nu.	Please pay me now.
Jeg sender Dem regningen.	I'll send you a bill.

FOR NUMBERS, see page 175

DOCTOR

Dentist

Can you recommend a good dentist?	**Kan De anbefale en god tandlæge?**	kehn dee ahnberfaaler ehn goadh **tahn**laier
Can I make an (urgent) appointment to see Doctor...?	**Kan jeg få en tid (hurtigst muligt) hos tandlæge...?**	kehn yigh faw ehn teedh (hoorteest mōōleet) hoass **tahn**laier
Can't you possibly make it earlier than that?	**Kan jeg ikke komme tidligere?**	kehn yigh **igger** koamer teedhl**ēē**errer
I've got toothache.	**Jeg har tandpine.**	yigh haar **tahn**pēēner
I've an abscess.	**Jeg har en byld.**	yigh haar ehn bewl
This tooth hurts.	**Jeg har ondt i denne tand.**	yigh haar oant ee **dehner** tahn
at the top	**foroven**	foro°°ern
at the bottom	**forneden**	forn**āy**dhern
in the front	**foran**	**for**ahn
at the back	**bagved**	**bah**vaydh
Can you fix it temporarily?	**Kan De behandle den midlertidigt?**	kehn dee ber**hahn**ler dehn **meedh**lerrteedheet
I don't want it extracted.	**Jeg vil ikke have den trukket ud.**	yigh veel **igger** hæ dehn **trooggert** ōōdh
I've a loose tooth.	**Jeg har en løs tand.**	yigh haar ehn lurss tahn
I've broken a tooth.	**Jeg har brækket en tand.**	yigh haar **brehg**gert ehn tahn
I've lost a filling.	**Jeg har tabt en plombe.**	yigh haar tahbt ehn **ploam**ber
The gum is very sore.	**Gummerne er meget ømme.**	**goom**merrner ayr **migh**ert urmer
The gum is bleeding.	**Gummerne bløder.**	**goom**merrner bl**ūr**dherr

Dentures

I've broken this denture.	**Jeg har brækket min protese.**	yigh haar **brehg**gert mēēn proat**āy**sser
Can you repair this denture?	**Kan De ordne denne protese?**	kehn dee **oard**ner **dehner** proat**āy**sser
What's it going to cost?	**Hvad vil det koste?**	vahdh veel day **koas**ter
When will it be ready?	**Hvornår kan den være færdig?**	vornawr kehn dehn **vǣ**rer færdee

Optician

I've broken my glasses.	**Mine briller er gået i stykker.**	mēēner breelerr ayr gawert ee stewggerr
Can you repair them for me?	**Kan De reparere dem for mig?**	kehn dee raypahrāyrer dehm foar migh
When will they be ready?	**Hvornår er de færdige?**	vornawr ayr dee færdēēer
Can you change the lenses?	**Kan De udskifte glassene?**	kehn dee ōōdhskeefter glahsserner
I want tinted lenses.	**Jeg ønsker tonede glas.**	yigh urnskerr toanerdher glahss
I've lost one of my contact lenses.	**Jeg har tabt en af mine kontaktlinser.**	yigh haar tahbt ehn ah mēēner koantahktleensserr
I'd like to buy a pair of binoculars.	**Jeg vil gerne købe en kikkert.**	yigh veel gehrner kūrber ehn kiggert
I'd like to buy a pair of sun-glasses.	**Jeg vil gerne købe et par solbriller.**	yigh veel gehrner kūrber eht pahr soalbrilerr
How much do I owe you?	**Hvor meget bliver det?**	vōar mighert blēēerr day
Do I pay you now or will you send me your bill?	**Skal jeg betale nu, eller sender De mig regningen?**	skahl yigh behtaaler noo ehlerr saynerr dee migh righneengern

Keeping fit

If you want to tone up those tired muscles, ask your hotel or local tourist office to direct you to a gymnasium or health institute.

Where can I find a...?	**Hvor kan jeg finde...?**	vōar kehn yigh finner
massage parlour	**et helseinstitut**	eht haylsserinsteetoot
physiotherapist	**en fysioterapeut**	ehn fewsseeoatayrahpoit
sauna	**en sauna**	ehn sownah
solarium	**et lysbehandlings- institut (højfjelds- sol)**	eht lewsberhahnleengs- insteetoot (hoifyaylssoal)
steam bath	**et dampbad**	eht dahmbaadh

FOR NUMBERS, see page 175

Reference section

Where do you come from?

Africa	**Afrika**	ahfrekaa
Asia	**Asien**	aassēēern
Australia	**Australien**	owstrahlēēern
Denmark	**Danmark**	dahnmahrk
England	**England**	ehnglahn
Europe	**Europa**	oiroapah
Finland	**Finland**	feenlahn
France	**Frankrig**	frahnkree
Germany	**Tyskland**	tewsklahn
Great Britain	**Storbritannien**	stoarbreetahnyern
Greenland	**Grønland**	grurnlahn
Iceland	**Island**	ēēslahn
India	**Indien**	indēēern
Ireland	**Irland**	eerlahn
Japan	**Japan**	yaapahn
New Zealand	**New Zealand**	"new zealand"
North America	**Nordamerika**	nōārahmehreekah
Norway	**Norge**	nōārger
Scotland	**Skotland**	skoatlahn
South Africa	**Sydafrika**	sēwdhahfreekah
South America	**Sydamerika**	sēwdhahmehreekah
Sweden	**Sverige**	svayrēēer
USA	**U.S.A.**	ooehssai
USSR	**Sovjetunionen**	so°°vaytooneeoanern
Wales	**Wales**	"wales"

And some important Danish cities and places:

Aalborg	**Ålborg**	awlboar
Aarhus	**Århus**	awrhōōss
Bornholm	**Bornholm**	boarnhoalm
Copenhagen	**København**	kurbernhown
Elsinore	**Helsingør**	haylseengūrr
Esbjerg	**Esbjerg**	ayssbyayr
Faroe Islands	**Færøerne**	fairūrerner
Frederikshaven	**Frederikshavn**	fraydherreekshown
Funen	**Fyn**	fewn
Jutland	**Jylland**	yewlahn
Middelfart	**Middelfart**	meedherlfahrt
Odense	**Odense**	oadhernsser
Roskilde	**Roskilde**	roaskeeller
Sealand	**Sjælland**	shehlahn

Numbers

0	nul	nool
1	en	ehn
2	to	toa
3	tre	tray
4	fire	feerer
5	fem	faym
6	seks	sayks
7	syv	sewv
8	otte	oader
9	ni	nee
10	ti	tee
11	elleve	aylver
12	tolv	toal
13	tretten	traydern
14	fjorten	fyoartern
15	femten	faymtern
16	seksten	sighstern
17	sytten	sewdern
18	atten	ahdern
19	nitten	needern
20	tyve	tewver
21	enogtyve	ehnotewver
22	toogtyve	toaotewver
23	treogtyve	trayotewver
24	fireogtyve	feererotewver
25	femogtyve	faymotewver
26	seksogtyve	sayksotewver
27	syvogtyve	sewvotewver
28	otteogtyve	oaderotewver
29	niogtyve	neeotewver
30.	tredive	traiver
31	enogtredive	ehnotraiver
32	toogtredive	toaotraiver
33	treogtredive	trayotraiver
40	fyrre	furrer
41	enogfyrre	ehnofurrer
42	toogfyrre	toaofurrer
43	treogfyrre	trayofurrer
50	halvtreds	hahltrayss
51	enoghalvtreds	ehnohahltrayss
52	tooghalvtreds	toaohahltrayss
53	treoghalvtreds	trayohahltrayss
60	tres	trayss
61	enogtres	ehnotrayss
62	toogtres	toaotrayss

63	treogtres	trayotrayss
70	halvfjerds	hahlfyayrss
71	enoghalvfjerds	ehnohahlfyayrss
72	tooghalvfjerds	toaohahlfyayrss
73	treoghalvfjerds	trayohahlfyayrss
80	firs	fēērss
81	enogfirs	ehnofēērss
82	toogfirs	toaofēērss
83	treogfirs	trayofēērss
90	halvfems	hahlfaymss
91	enoghalvfems	ehnohahlfaymss
92	tooghalvfems	toaohahlfaymss
93	treoghalvfems	trayohahlfaymss
100	hundrede	hoonrerdher
101	hundrede og et	hoonrerdher o eht
102	hundrede og to	hoonrerdher o toa
110	hundrede og ti	hoonrerdher o tee
120	hundrede og tyve	hoonrerdher o tēwver
130	hundrede og tredive	hoonrerdher o traiver
140	hundrede og fyrre	hoonrerdher o fūrrer
150	hundrede og halvtreds	hoonrerdher o hahltrayss
160	hundrede og tres	hoonrerdher o trays
170	hundrede og halvfjerds	hoonrerdher o hahlfyayrss
180	hundrede og firs	hoonrerdher o fēērss
190	hundrede og halvfems	hoonrerdher o hahlfaymss
200	to hundrede	toa hoonrerdher
300	tre hundrede	tray hoonrerdher
400	fire hundrede	fēērer hoonrerdher
500	fem hundrede	faym hoonrerdher
600	seks hundrede	sayks hoonrerdher
700	syv hundrede	sewv hoonrerdher
800	otte hundrede	oader hoonrerdher
900	ni hundrede	nee hoonrerdher
1000	tusind	tōōsseen
1100	et tusind et hundrede	eht tōōsseen eht hoonrerdher
1200	et tusind to hundrede	eht tōōsseen toa hoonrerdher
2000	to tusind	toa tōōsseen
5000	fem tusind	faym tōōsseen
10,000	ti tusind	tee tōōsseen
50,000	halvtreds tusind	hahltrayss tōōsseen
100,000	hundrede tusind	hoonrerdher tōōsseen
1,000,000	en million	ehn meelyoan
1,000,000,000	en milliard	ehn meelyahrd

first	**første**	furrster
second	**anden**	ahnern
third	**tredje**	trāÿer
fourth	**fjerde**	fyehrer
fifth	**femte**	faymter
sixth	**sjette**	syayder
seventh	**syvende**	sēwverner
eighth	**ottende**	oaderner
ninth	**niende**	nēēerner
tenth	**tiende**	tēēerner
once	**én gang**	ehn gahng
twice	**to gange**	toa gahnger
three times	**tre gange**	tray gahnger
a half	**en halv**	ehn hahl
half of (the book)	**halvdelen (af bogen)**	hahldehlern (ah bōāern)
half a (page)	**en halv (side)**	ehn hahl (sēēdher)
a quarter	**en kvart**	ehn kvahrt
three-quarters	**tre kvart**	tray kvahrt
a third	**en tredjedel**	ehn trayerdehl
two-thirds	**to tredjedele**	toa trayerdehler
a pair of	**et par**	eht pahr
a dozen	**et dusin**	eht doossēēn
1983	**nitten hundrede og treogfirs**	needernhoonrerdher oa trayofeerss
1984	**nitten hundrede og fireogfirs**	needernhoonrerdher oa feererofeerss
1985	**nitten hundrede og femogfirs**	needernhoonrerdher oa faymofeerss
1990	**nitten hundrede og halvfems**	needernhoonrerdher oa hahlfaymss

Time

et kvarter over tolv
(eht kvahr**tehr** o^{oo}er toal)

tyve minutter over ét
(**t$\overline{\text{ew}}$**ver mee**nood**err o^{oo}er eht)

femogtyve minutter over to
(**faym**ot$\overline{\text{ew}}$ver mee**nood**err o^{oo}er toa)

halv fire
(hahl **f$\overline{\text{ee}}$r**er)

femogtyve minutter i fem
(**faym**ot$\overline{\text{ew}}$ver mee**nood**err ee faym)

tyve minutter i seks
(**t$\overline{\text{ew}}$**ver mee**nood**err ee sayks)

et kvarter i syv
(eht kvahr**tehr** ee sewv)

ti minutter i otte
(tee mee**nood**err ee **oad**er)

fem minutter i ni
(faym mee**nood**err ee nee)

ti
(tee)

fem minutter over elleve
(faym mee**nood**err o^{oo}er **ayl**ver)

ti minutter over tolv
(tee mee**nood**err o^{oo}er toal)

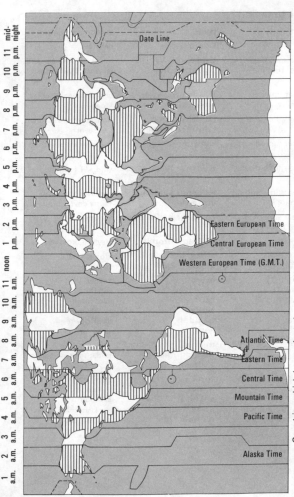

Countries which have adopted a time differing from that in the corresponding time zone. Note that also in the USSR, official time is one hour ahead of the time in each corresponding time zone. In summer, numerous countries advance time one hour ahead of standard time.

REFERENCE SECTION

1 a.m. 2 a.m. 3 a.m. 4 a.m. 5 a.m. 6 a.m. 7 a.m. 8 a.m. 9 a.m. 10 a.m. 11 a.m. noon 1 p.m. 2 p.m. 3 p.m. 4 p.m. 5 p.m. 6 p.m. 7 p.m. 8 p.m. 9 p.m. 10 p.m. 11 p.m. mid-night

Date Line

Eastern European Time
Central European Time
Western European Time (G.M.T.)

Atlantic Time
Eastern Time
Central Time
Mountain Time
Pacific Time

Alaska Time

What time is it?

What time is it?	**Hvad er klokken?**	vahdh ayr **kloaggern**
It's...	**Den er...**	dehn ayr
Excuse me. Can you tell me the time?	**Undskyld. Vil De sige mig, hvad klokken er?**	oonskewl. veel dee **sēēer** migh vahdh **kloaggern** ayr
I'll meet you at... tomorrow.	**Vi ses i morgen klokken...**	vee **sāyss** ee **mōāern** **kloaggern**
I'm sorry I'm late.	**Undskyld, jeg kommer for sent.**	oonskewl yigh **koamer** foar saynt
At what time does... open?	**Hvornår åbner...?**	vornawr awbnerr
At what time does... close?	**Hvornår lukker...?**	vornawr loogger
At what time should I be there?	**Hvornår skal jeg være der?**	vornawr skahl yigh **vǣrer** dayr
At what time will you be there?	**Hvornår er De der?**	vornawr ayr dee dayr
Can I come...?	**Må jeg komme...?**	may yigh **koamer**
at 8 o'clock	**klokken 8**	**kloaggern** 8
at 2.30	**klokken 2.30**	**kloaggern** 2.30
after (prep.)	**efter**	ehfterr
afterwards	**bagefter**	bahehfterr
before	**før/foran**	fūrr/foarahn
early	**tidlig**	teedhlee
in time	**til tiden**	til **tēēdhern**
late	**sent**	saynt
midnight	**midnat**	midnaht
noon	**middag/midt på dagen**	midai/mit paw **daiern**
hour	**time**	**tēēmer**
minute	**minut**	meenood
second	**sekund**	**sāykoon**
quarter of an hour	**et kvarter**	eht kvah**rtehr**
half an hour	**en halv time**	ehn hahl **tēēmer**

Days

What day is it today?	**Hvilken dag er det i dag?**	vilkern dai ayr day ee dai
Sunday	**søndag**	surndai
Monday	**mandag**	mahndai
Tuesday	**tirsdag**	tēērsdai
Wednesday	**onsdag**	oansdai
Thursday	**torsdag**	toarsdai
Friday	**fredag**	fraydai
Saturday	**lørdag**	lūrdai

Note: The names of days and months are not capitalized in Denmark.

in the morning	**om morgenen**	oam mōaernern
during the day	**i løbet af dagen**	ee lūrbert ah daiern
in the afternoon	**om eftermiddagen**	oam ehfterrmidaiern
in the evening	**om aftenen**	oam ahfternern
at night	**om natten**	oam nahdern
the day before yesterday	**i forgårs**	ee foargawrss
yesterday	**i går**	ee gawr
today	**i dag**	ee dai
tomorrow	**i morgen**	ee mōaern
the day after tomorrow	**i overmorgen**	ee o°°ermōaern
the day before	**dagen før**	daiern fūrr
the following day	**den følgende dag**	dehn furlyerner dai
two days ago	**for to dage siden**	foar toa daier sēēdhern
in three days' time	**om tre dage**	oam tray daier
last week	**i sidste uge**	ee seester ōōer
next week	**i næste uge**	ee nehster ōōer
for a fortnight (two weeks)	**i fjorten dage (i to uger)**	ee fyoartern daier (ee toa ōōer)
birthday	**fødselsdag**	fūrrserlsdai
day	**dag**	dai
day off	**fridag**	freedai
holiday	**helligdag**	hayleedai
holidays	**ferie**	fehrēēer
month	**måned**	mawnerdh
school holidays	**skoleferie**	skoalerfehrēēer
vacation	**ferie**	fehrēēer
week	**uge**	ōōer
weekday	**ugedag**	ōōerdai
weekend	**weekend**	"weekend"

Months

January	januar	jahnooahr
February	februar	fehbrooahr
March	marts	mahrss
April	april	ahpr**ee**l
May	maj	migh
June	juni	y**oo**nee
July	juli	y**oo**lee
August	august	owgoost
September	september	sehptaymberr
October	oktober	oaktoaberr
November	november	noavaymberr
December	december	dehsaymberr

since June	siden juni	s**ee**dhern y**oo**nee
during the month of August	i løbet af august måned	ee l**ur**bert ah owgoost mawnerdh
last month	i sidste måned	ee seester mawnerdh
next month	i næste måned	ee nehster mawnerdh
the month before	måneden før	mawnerdhern f**ur**r
the following month	måneden efter	mawnerdhern ehfterr

| July 1 | første juli | furrsterr y**oo**lee |
| March 17 | syttende marts | sewderner mahrss |

Letter headings are written thus:

Copenhagen, August 17, 19..   **København, den 17. august 19..**

Odense, July 1, 19..   **Odense, den 1. juli 19..**

Seasons

spring	forår	foarawr
summer	sommer	soamerr
autumn	efterår	ehfterrawr
winter	vinter	veenterr

in spring	om foråret	oam foarawrert
during the summer	i løbet af sommeren	ee l**ur**bert ah soamerrern
last autumn	sidste efterår	seester ehfterrawr
next winter	næste vinter, til vinter	nehster veenterr, til veenterr

Public holidays

Though Denmark's banks, offices and major shops close on public holidays, museums and tourist attractions will be open, if on reduced hours. It will also be business as usual in the cafés.

January 1	New Year
June 5	Constitution Day (afternoon only)
December 24, 25, 26	(afternoon only) Christmas
Movable dates:	Maundy Thursday Good Friday Easter Monday Prayer Day (4th Friday after Easter) Ascension Day Whit Monday

The year round...

Here are the average temperatures for some Danish cities in degrees Fahrenheit:

	Copenhagen	Odense (Funen)	Aalborg (Jutland)	Sandvig (Bornholm)
January	32.2	32.2	31.1	32.9
February	31.8	31.8	30.4	32.0
March	35.4	35.6	34.4	34.3
April	43.9	44.1	42.3	41.2
May	53.2	52.7	51.4	48.6
June	60.0	58.8	57.6	57.4
July	64.0	62.2	61.5	62.6
August	63.1	61.5	60.6	62.8
September	57.0	55.8	54.7	57.4
October	48.7	47.8	46.4	49.5
November	41.7	41.2	39.9	42.3
December	36.5	36.3	35.2	37.1

Common abbreviations

adr.	adresse	address
afs.	afsender	from (on a letter)
A/S	aktieselskab	Ltd.
bem.	bemærk	please note
bl.a.	blandt andet	among other things
co.	kompagni	company
D	Damer	Ladies
DFDS	De Forenede Dampskibs-selskaber	United Danish Shipping Companies
DK	Danmark	Denmark
DSB	De Danske Statsbaner	Danish State Railways
d.v.s.	det vil sige	that is
EF	Det Europæiska Økonomiske Fællesskab	European Economic Community (Common Market)
FDM	De Forenede Danske Motorejere	Danish Automobile Club
f.eks.	for eksempel	for example
FN	De Forenede Nationer	United Nations
frk.	frøken	Miss
p.t.	for tiden	now
H	Herrer	Gentlemen
hk	hestekræfter	horsepower
hr.	herre	Mr.
ing.	ingeniør	engineer
i.st.f.	i stedet for	instead of
jfr.	jævnfør	see
KDAK	Kongelig Dansk Automobil Klub	Royal Danish Automobil Club
kr.	kroner	crowns
L.	lille	small (in conn. towns)
maks.	maksimum	maximum
min.	minimum	minimum
m.m.	med mere	and so on
nr.	nummer	number
o.s.v.	og så videre	and so on
p.gr.af	på grund af	because of
s.	sal	floor
St.	Store	big (in conn. towns)
skt.	Sankt	Saint
sml.	sammenlign	compare
t.h.	til højre	at right
t.v.	til venstre	at left
v.s.a.	ved siden af	beside

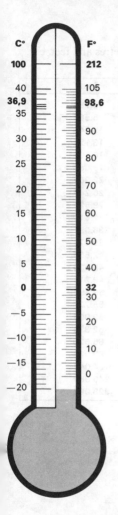

Conversion tables

Centimetres and inches

To change centimetres into inches, multiply by 0.39.

To change inches into centimetres, multiply by 2.54.

	in.	feet	yards
1 mm	0,039	0,003	0,001
1 cm	0,39	0,03	0,01
1 dm	3,94	0,32	0,10
1 m	39,40	3,28	1,09

	mm	cm	m
1 in.	25,4	2,54	0,025
1 ft.	304,8	30,48	0,304
1 yd.	914,4	91,44	0,914

(32 metres = 35 yards)

Temperature

To convert centigrade into degrees Fahrenheit, multiply centigrade by 1.8 and add 32.

To convert degrees Fahrenheit into centigrade, subtract 32 from Fahrenheit and divide by 1.8.

Metres and feet

The figure in the middle stands for both metres and feet, e.g.
1 metre = 3.28 feet and 1 foot = 0.30 m.

Metres		Feet
0.30	1	3.281
0.61	2	6.563
0.91	3	9.843
1.22	4	13.124
1.52	5	16.403
1.83	6	19.686
2.13	7	22.967
2.44	8	26.248
2.74	9	29.529
3.05	10	32.810
3.35	11	36.091
3.66	12	39.372
3.96	13	42.635
4.27	14	45.934
4.57	15	49.215
4.88	16	52.496
5.18	17	55.777
5.49	18	59.058
5.79	19	62.339
6.10	20	65.620
7.62	25	82.023
15.24	50	164.046
22.86	75	246.069
30.48	100	328.092

Other conversion charts

REFERENCE SECTION

Weight conversion

The figure in the middle stands for both kilograms and pounds, e.g. 1 kilogram = 2.20 lb. and 1 lb. = 0.45 kilograms.

Kilograms (kg)		Avoirdupois pounds
0.45	1	2.205
0.90	2	4.405
1.35	3	6.614
1.80	4	8.818
2.25	5	11.023
2.70	6	13.227
3.15	7	15.432
3.60	8	17.636
4.05	9	19.840
4.50	10	22.045
6.75	15	33.068
9.00	20	44.889
11.25	25	55.113
22.50	50	110.225
33.75	75	165.338
45.00	100	220.450

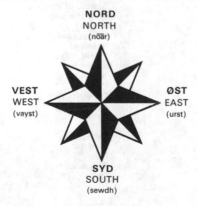

NORD
NORTH
(noār)

VEST
WEST
(vayst)

ØST
EAST
(urst)

SYD
SOUTH
(sewdh)

What does that sign mean?

You're sure to encounter some of these signs or notices on your trip!

Adgang forbudt for uvedkommende	No trespassing
Cykelsti	Cycle path
Damer	Ladies
Døren er åben	Enter without knocking
Elevator	Lift (elevator)
Fare	Danger
...forbudt	...forbidden
Fri adgang	Entrance free
Fri/ledig	Vacant
Giv agt	Caution
Herrer	Gentlemen
Indgang	Entrance
Ingen adgang	No entrance
Ikke rygere	No smoking
Kasse	Cashier's
Kold	Cold
Livsfare	Danger of death
Lukket	Closed
Må ikke berøres	Do not touch
Nødudgang	Emergency exit
Oplysning	Information
Optaget	Occupied
Pas på hunden	Beware of the dog
Pas på trinet	Mind the step
Privat	Private
Privatvej	Private road
Reserveret	Reserved
Ring	Please ring
Rygere	Smoking
Rygning forbudt	No smoking
Skub	Push
Til leje	To let, for hire
Til salg	For sale
Træk	Pull
Udgang	Exit
Udsalg	Sales
Udsolgt	Sold out
Varm	Hot
Vent	Please wait
Åben	Open

Emergency

The all-purpose emergency number is 000, and called from public phone boxes it's free—coins are not needed. Ask for police, fire or ambulance as required. Speak distinctly (English will be understood) and state your number and location.

Be quick	**Hurtig**	hoortee
Call the police	**Tilkald politiet**	tilkahl poaleetēēert
CAREFUL	**FORSIGTIG**	forseegtee
Come here	**Kom her**	koam hayr
Come in	**Kom ind**	koam een
Danger	**Fare**	faarer
FIRE	**BRAND/ILD**	brahn/eel
Gas	**Gas**	gahss
Get a doctor	**Tilkald en læge**	tilkahl ehn laier
Go away	**Forsvind**	forsveen
HELP	**HJÆLP**	yehlp
Get help quickly	**Tilkald hjælp—hurtigt**	tilkahl yehlp—hoorteet
I'm ill	**Jeg er syg**	yigh ayr sew
I'm lost	**Jeg er faret vild**	yigh ayr faarert veel
I've lost my...	**Jeg har tabt min...**	yigh haar tahbt mēēn
Keep your hands to yourself	**Pas Dem selv**	pahss dehm sayl
Leave me alone	**Lad mig være**	lahdh migh værer
Lie down	**Læg Dem ned**	lehg dehm naydh
Listen	**Hør**	hurr
Listen to me	**Hør hvad jeg siger**	hurr vahdh yigh sēēer
LOOK	**SE**	sāy
Look out	**Giv agt**	gee ahgt
POLICE	**POLITI**	poaleetee
Quick	**Hurtig**	hoortee
STOP	**STOP/STANDS**	stoab/stahnss
Stop here	**Stands her**	stahnss hayr
Stop that man	**Stands den mand**	stahnss dehn mahn
Stop thief	**Stop tyven**	stoab tēwvern

FOR CAR ACCIDENTS, see page 150

REFERENCE SECTION

Index

Quick reference page

Please.	**Vær venlig...**	vær **vehn**lee
Thank you.	**Tak.**	tæk
Yes/No.	**Ja/Nej**	yæ/nigh
Excuse me.	**Undskyld**	**oon**skewl
Waiter, please.	**Tjener!**	ty**ay**nerr
How much is that?	**Hvad koster det?**	vahdh **koa**sterr day
Where are the toilets?	**Hvor er toiletterne?**	vo̅ar ayr toaee**lay**derrner

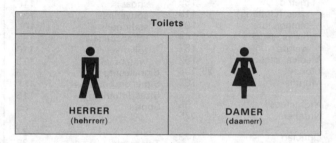

Toilets

HERRER
(**hehr**rerr)

DAMER
(**daa**merr)

Could you tell me...?	**Kan De sige mig...?**	kehn dee **se̅e̅**er migh
where/when/why	**hvor/hvornår/** **hvorfor**	vo̅ar/vor**nawr**/**vor**for
Help me, please.	**Vær venlig at** **hjælpe mig.**	vær **vehn**lee aht **yehl**per migh
What time is it?	**Hvad er klokken?**	vahdh ayr **kloag**gern
Where is the... consulate?	**Hvor er det...** **konsulat?**	vo̅ar ayr day... konso**olaat**
American British Canadian	**amerikanske** **engelske** **canadiske**	ahmehree**kaan**sker **ehng**erlsker kah**naa**disker
What does this mean? I don't understand.	**Hvad betyder dette?** **Jeg forstår det ikke.**	vahdh ber**te̅w**dherr **dehd**der yigh for**stawr** day **igg**er
Do you speak English?	**Taler De engelsk?**	**tail**err dee **ehng**erlsk